I0170088

HOW THE

cancer

FELL OUT

OF ME

by

Yogi Sally Ann Slight

ALL RIGHTS RESERVED.
NO PART OF THIS PUBLICATION MAY BE REPRODUCED,
STORED IN A RETRIEVAL SYSTEM, OR TRANSMITTED IN ANY FORM
OR BY ANY MEANS, ELECTRONIC, MECHANICAL,
PHOTOCOPYING OR OTHERWISE
WITHOUT THE PRIOR PERMISSION OF THE COPYRIGHT OWNER.

© COPYRIGHT 2020

SAS PUBLISHING.

DARTMOUTH, DEVON,

UNITED KINGDOM

Tel: 01803 363855

ALL RIGHTS RESERVED

ISBN 978-1910123-522

With the greatest of respect and thanks to...

'Christian Science'
Mary Baker Eddy

Sivananda Yoga Ashram, Bahamas

Dr Ihaleakala Hew Len
&
Dr Joe Vitale

Dr David Hawkins

HOW THE

cancer

FELL OUT

OF ME

* Where have you been for all these months?

Getting over cancer thanks.

* ...was it terrible?

No, I actually used the skills I had learnt when I was at the Yoga Ashram and the many books on alternative Healthcare that I have read, but they never told me there would be a lot of pain, and it felt like someone was putting their hands inside me and ripping my womb out, but I passed out long enough to not feel it anymore, and the next day, I was sitting on the sofa, I felt a huge movement and it just fell out of me! I put it in a jar and took it to the Doctors.....'There you go, look what I made,' .....and I have felt fantastic ever since July 2017.

* it fell out of you?

Yes, thankfully it was in my womb, so it could fall out of me!

* But how could that happen?

Well, I hadn't felt right for quite some time, and I had been to the Hospital to get my bits checked out the year before.

* Yes, I remember that, and they told you it was a bit rough up there but nothing to worry about.

Yes, that's right, the nurse told me that, and I went home. But they called me back months later, asking why I hadn't waited to talk to the Doctor about my results. So I went back and had another internal, and this time I waited to speak to the Doctor who also had a look and did a small operation there, and she said she had removed something. But I still didn't feel like I do now!....and the bleeding was still very bad, and that was what I was taking medication for....to stop the bleeding.

* So how did things change from that?

A few months later I was doing some self reflexology on my feet and found a big black mark on the sole of my foot....I knew it was something inside my body so I had to get guidance, as I didn't want to keep going to Hospital.

* You went back to the Doctors?

No, I sat and asked God, and I was guided back to Mary Baker Eddy's book, 'Christian Science'. I had read it about 5 years ago and it didn't really mean anything to me, I accepted it's teaching but it was way over my head.
* You didn't understand it?

Yes, I understood it, but I felt it wasn't relevant to me, I was looking to make loads of money at the time and wanted guidance for that......but this time the book opened at the page I needed, and I read what I needed to know.

* And what was that?

On page 410 under the title, MENTAL TREATMENT ILLUSTRATED I found,
Disease does not exist?....It is only your thoughts that create what you experience!   If mental practice is abused or is used in any way except to promote right thinking and doing, the power to heal mentally will diminish, until the practitioner's healing ability is wholly lost. 'Be not afraid! Said Job: 'The thing which I had greatly feared is come upon me.'.........If the student silently called the disease by name, when he argued against it, as a general rule the body would respond more quickly - just as a person replies more readily when his name is spoken; but this was the student was not perfectly attuned to divine Science, and needed the arguments of truth for reminders. If Spirit or the power of divine Love bear witness to the truth, this is the ultimatum, the scientific way, and the healing is instantaneous.

* But how could that help you?

Well, lets take the first part of that excerpt.....*If mental practice is abused...*
When you fear something and think about it alot, you create what you fear and experience it.

* So you feared cancer and got it?

So it seems, but in a subtle way rather than outwardly speaking of it. When I look back on my life my deepest sadness was with my kids being taken from me, and even though I covered my sadness outwardly, deep inside it kept growing and so it had to grow in the place where they came from.....but a place where it could be released easily, well easier than surgery it seems.

* So, you grew the cancer?

Yes, over many years of deep sadness.

* But that doesn't help me to understand how it could fall out of you?

Well, I had to understand it!....you weren't growing it, I was...it was my doing, so I had to undo it....and the moment I understood what I had done, I was vibrating at a higher frequency, and so the negative mass was not able to stay within me any longer.....I was forgiving myself, and so raising myself to a higher level of understanding, and in that understanding nothing can harm me....except myself of course, ...and I had already done that!

* But I still don't understand how it can fall out of you.

No, neither do I, but I am so glad it did......and since then I have been learning so much more about what I do to my body by way of my negative thinking.

* What else have you learnt?

That Dementia and all disease is also just a matter of wrongful thinking and that can be turned around too!

* How on earth can you turn around the breakdown of cells in the brain, by thinking?

Because that's where the thinking comes from....so it means if you're thinking is horrid, so will be the outcome of your thinking!.....*and the ability to heal is wholly lost*, as it says in the book.

* But what does that mean?

The next paragraph says....*It is recorded that once Jesus asked the name of a disease, a disease which moderns would call Dementia.* And this book was 1st published in 1890, so it has been known about for along time now!

* So why has there been more people with Dementia?

Because they have been thinking and not knowing what their thinking was creating for themselves!.....Don't you remember when you used to think horrid thoughts about what you would like to happen to other people?.....and then horrid things happened to you!

* I still do haha!....but I will try a bit harder not to now!

.....well, we find out more in the next paragraph......
The demon, or evil, replied that his name was Legion (just like negative thoughts, there are many of them). *Thereupon Jesus cast out the evil, and the insane man was changed and straight away became whole. The Scripture seems to import that Jesus caused the evil to be self-seen and so destroyed.*
Jesus knew what He was dealing with and so could see the best for the man.
Just like what happened to me with the cancer! I realized that I had created it by my negative thoughts, sadness and non-forgiveness of my past.....And also, I was taught that we are all one, and reflections of ourselves, therefore, Jesus saw Himself in that man and wanted to heal Himself....and so He did!...and so I do!
* But how does Jesus heal someone of Dementia by seeing Himself in him?

Well, you have to know the rules and Principles of Life......that is what He was sent here to do for us, teach us the rules, so we can look after ourselves!

* So why don't we know the rules and Principles?

People don't like change when it means they lose power over another person, and Jesus was just reminding everyone of what they are, Self-Healers and Perfection.....we have just forgotten this information over the years, as there have been so many other things to think about, rather than think about the good.

* So how can I heal myself of Dementia?

Do you have it?

* No, not yet?

If you think that way you are planting seeds that will blossom later.... is that how you think you life will be in the future....full of disease and suffering?

* I hope not!

Then you have to start thinking that you are perfect, that you are thankful for all the good things you have, enjoy every moment and smile.....it is your choice!

* Is that all I have to do?

Yes, and then go and find something good to do with your time here.

* How can that be true?

Because I too have had the feeling of losing my mind, in the time of all the internal disease....I had felt my mind had been blurring and I found myself at a bus station, and I just didn't know what to do and what bus to get on.....so I just started to thank Jesus for my perfect health, over and over again, I left my mind in His hands, and since that day, I have such a clarity in my mind, it is wonderful.....but it was the next paragraph that really helped me to understand this....

* OK, what does it say?

This is the best bit.....*The procuring cause and foundation of all sickness is fear, ignorance, or sin. Disease is always induced by a false sense mentally entertained, not destroyed. Disease is an image of thought externalized. The mental state is called a material state. Whatever is cherished in mortal mind as the physical condition is imaged forth on the body.*

* So you understood you had had, bad thoughts?

Yes.

* And when you realized that, that is when the cancer fell out of you?

No, I had to mentally/physically change my mind about my disease.

* And how did you do that?

By reading the next paragraph......*Always begin your treatment by allaying the fear of patients. Silently reassure them as to their exemption from disease and danger. Watch the result of this simple rule of Christian Science, and you will find that it alleviates the symptoms of every disease. If you succeed in wholly removing the fear, your patient is healed. The great fact that God lovingly governs all, never punishing aught but sin, is your stand point, from which to advance and destroy the human fear of sickness.*

And I was my own patient, so I had to destroy my own fear of sickness, as I knew no one better than myself to do that.....When I KNEW I was exempt from disease and danger, that was when I felt the pain....oh what a huge and terrible pain it was in my stomach, and as I said, it felt like someone putting their hands inside of me and ripping out my insides.....so I passed out in the pain.

* So are you going to recommend this treatment to your clients?

I can only tell my story....If clients want to change their mind and Master their thinking, then they too could feel this good!.......AND STOP THE SICKNESS!

* So you really think you are healed now?

YES!....I feel fantastic, my thoughts are now more lovely and I am in happiness, so it is a choice anyone can take.....but it's always better when you know someone else has been through the same experience so you can get helpful advice, if you cannot figure it out for yourself....although we all have that ability too!......I had just lost my way for a while, and now I am back on track and doing the best I can with everything I have left in my life....and for that I am truly thankful.

* And what are you going to do now?

I am going to help more people understand that disease is a choice!

Everything that is today, could not be,
if it were not for that,
which was before.

HOW TO MEDITATE CORRECTLY,
TO GET THE HIGHEST LEVEL OF UNDERSTANDING
FROM THIS WORK...

Sit,
Be still,
Shut your eyes (after reading this of course!)
SMILE...

Take your time...

FEEL every aspect of that Smile on your face...

the stretched lips over your teeth
your teeth gently rest upon each other
your cheeks lifted upwards and tensing the muscles
your eyes closed and rested
your forehead is relaxed
your ears are pushed out a little by the uplifting of the cheeks
your neck is relaxed
and your shoulders are released and resting...

this FEELS GOOD...
be THANKFUL for this GOOD SMILE

Revel in this FEELING of GOODNESS

so THANKFUL for FEELING GOOD

Now, send that Smile deep into your tummy...
your tummy is smiling
your face is still smiling
your eyes are closed

and you FEEL that smile deep within your tummy...

Spread that GOOD FEELING into every cell of your body,
so that each cell and molecule is refreshed in GOODNESS

The more your face smiles the brighter the FEELING becomes within you.

You can FEEL the Energy move within every cell throughout the body...
there is a gentle pulsing of the GOOD FEELING...

(do not force this...it comes to you over time)

Trust the process of the SMILE

Trust the process of the FEELING of GOODNESS

You are focused on the process of FEELING GOOD......
.
.
.
.

.
You have been rewarded with GOOD FEELING
You FEEL GOOD
.
You are now on the same LEVEL as Source

.
.
.

.
You may now ASK

.

.

.

.

.

You may now LISTEN

.

.

.

.

.

You now KNOW

.

.

.

.

To spend time on reaching God/Source, is time well spent.

Never hurry to God/Source with your request
Allow yourself to shine from FEELING GOOD

You will be noticed
You will be heard
You will be Healed...

You are Loved.

Peace be with you

Yogi Sally Ann Slight

P'RAISE
the Universal Law'd
of
unConditional
LOVE

The PREVENTION of dementia

BY READING THIS BOOK
YOU WILL CHANGE YOUR LIFE FOR THE BETTER
AND ONLY IF YOU WANT TO.

AS WITH ALL OF LIFE
YOU HAVE THE CHOICE.

WHEN YOU UNDERSTAND AND TRUST
THAT YOU WANT TO CHANGE YOUR LIFE FOR THE BETTER
THEN YOU CAN DO IT
FOR YOURSELF
BECAUSE NO ONE ELSE CAN ACTUALLY HELP YOU
UNLESS YOU WANT THEM TO TELL YOU HOW.

AND
WHEN YOU TRUST
WHEN YOU BELIEVE
WHEN YOU WANT TO

YOU CAN ACHIEVE ANYTHING

UNIVERSAL LAW

7 Keys that Affect Reality and Good Health.

Everything in the Universe obeys the same Laws.
These natural laws govern creation and existence.

They are consistent and they are everywhere,
and each one holds an important key to creating balance
and harmony within yourself and your life's experiences.

When you understand these 7 laws
and apply them to your daily living,
you learn to control yourself,
your environment and everything in it.

To begin, it is important to state that
the first 3 of the Universal Laws of the Universe are...
IMMUTABLE
meaning they cannot be changed.
Unchanging over time.

And the last 4 are...
MUTABLE
liable to change, changeable.

Each of these Laws exist in nature and work directly with our
Mental, Emotional, Spiritual and *Physical* states.

By understanding and implementing these laws,
you have the wisdom to take charge of your life,
influence your environment
and direct your personal journey.

The 1st Law is the
LAW of MENTALISM

This Law states that all is Mind, the Universe is mental.

Everything we see and experience in our physical world
originates from the invisible mental realm.

This governs all outward manifestations in our material world.

Everything that is apparent to our physical senses is in actuality Spirit,
and that Spirit is One Universal Consciousness or Mind.

What appears to be separate is actually connected,
everything you think and therefore do,
is an interaction of thought with thought.

Through the power of your mind, you influence your existence.

Your thought also has an effect on an energetic level,
your mind is a part of the one Universal Mind
and your reality is a manifestation of your mind.

All of the world, and or Universe
is a manifestation existing in the Mind of the All,
or more simply stated,
the underlying reality of the Universe is Mind.

This Law allows the person to use the other Laws to effect change.

The 2nd Law is the
LAW of CORRESPONDENCE

This embodies the truth that there is
Harmony, Agreement and Correspondence
between the
Spiritual, Mental and Physical realms.

As above, so below.
As below, so above.
As within, so without.
As without, so within.

There is no separation because everything within the Universe
resides in the One Universal Mind.

The same pattern is expressed on all planes of existence
from the smallest electron to the largest planet and vice versa.

Therefore, there is always correspondence
between the Laws and the various planes of existence.

The Energetic and Spiritual plane
directly corresponds with the Physical plane,
and the Energy you project with your Physical body,
via your Thoughts, Beliefs and Emotions,
directly correspond with the Spiritual realm.

This law enables a person to reason intelligently
from the known to the unknown,
meaning you can use your individual mind
to reach into the other areas of the Universal Mind,
to find solutions to any, or all, perceived difficulties.

The 3rd Law is the
LAW of VIBRATION

The Law of Vibration states that nothing rests,
everything moves,
everything vibrates.

The whole Universe is vibration,
everything we experience through our Physical senses
is in fact vibration.

The difference between the different manifestations of
Mind, Matter and Energy
largely results from varying states of vibration.

For example...
Sound is Light at a lower vibration
&
Light is Sound at a high oscillation.

Thoughts and emotions are also vibrations
and the Law of Attraction itself has it's foundation in this Law.

Understanding vibration and frequency,
and learning to control mental vibrations at will,
gives a person the unique power to have authority over their reality.

.

.

.

.

.

"Make a decision and then make the decision right.
Line up your Energy with it.
In most cases, it doesn't really matter what you decide.
Just decide.
There are endless options that would serve you enormously well,
and all or any one of them is better than no decision."

The 4th Law is the
LAW of POLARITY

This is the first of the 'Mutable Laws' and it states,
everything is dual,
everything has poles,
everything has its pairs of opposites.

Like and unlike are the same,
opposites are identical in nature but different in degree.

Extremes meet.
All Truths are but half truths.
All paradox's may be reconciled.
*(A paradox is a statement that may seem contradictory
but can be true, or at least make sense...
Save money, by spending it.
If I know one thing, it's that I know nothing...etc)*

In everything there are 2 poles or opposite aspects.
Opposites are actually the same thing,
they vary only in degree.
They are in fact identical in nature,
they are the 2 extreme sides of the very same thing.

Love & hate,
Black & White,
Hot & Cold,
Peace & war,
Light & darkness
and even
Energy & Matter.

Just as you have the ability to transform
your Thoughts and Emotions from hate to Love,
you can equally transform your Energy into Matter.

It is a Universal law.

We can change our perception of the degree of an opposite,
by recognizing that it has that degree.

In other words,
you can choose that any perceived difficulty
you currently have in your life,
is but only one degree of something else,
something that actually has the opposite of that.

There are different expressions of the same thing,
and because you already have one of them,
you only need to focus and change your energy
to be fixated on another degree of that.

It is not an obstacle that needs to be overcome,
rather it is something you already have
that you only need to choose which degree to focus on.

<u>ENLIGHTENMENT</u>
PEACE
JOY
LOVE
REASON
ACCEPTANCE
WILLINGNESS
Neutrality
Courage
Pride
Anger
desire
fear
grief
apathy
guilt
shame

"The opposite of any perceived difficulty
already exists as a part of it.
In every perceived failure lies success.
It is only a matter of varying degree."

The 5th Law is the
LAW of RHYTHM

This Law states that everything flows, out and in.
Everything has its tides, all things rise and fall.

The pendulum swing manifests in everything,
the measure of the swing to the right
is the measure of the swing to the left.

Rhythm compensates.

We can easily see this Law in Action
with the tides of the ocean,
in business trends and cycles,
life and death,
creation and destruction,
and even how our Thoughts can move
from Positive to negative and back again.

Nothing stops, it is always changing.

This is another 'Mutable Law'.

When a person understands this Law they can polarize
to the degree of the swing that they desire on the pendulum,
to keep from being swung back to the other extreme.

To do this you must become aware of the subtle swing back
in a movement and not allow discouragement or fear to set in.

Keep your thoughts focused on your outcome,
as in the example given in the Law of Polarity...
and remain consistent in your endeavours,
no matter how far back this transitory Law pulls you.

And most reassuring is, that this Law states
that you must be pulled back to the other side in doing so.

The 6th Law is the
LAW of CAUSE & EFFECT

Every Cause has its Effect.
Every Effect has it's Cause.

Everything happens according to the Law.

Chance is but a name for, 'Law Not Recognized'.

There are many planes of Causation, but nothing escapes the Law.

Every Effect that is seen in the outside physical world,
has a very specific Cause,
which has it's origin in the inner Mental world.

As this is another 'Mutable Law'.

The Conscious Creator makes the conscious choice
to rise above any circumstance they no longer wish to experience.

They choose the degree or expression to focus upon,
they recognise the swing of the Rhythm,
and remain steadfast,
and they become the Cause that creates the Effect they choose.

They know that the Law of Cause & Effect begins on the Spiritual plane,
where everything is instantaneous.

Having this awareness,
gives the Conscious Creator,
the ability to rule their own plane.

"What you put in, will determine what you get back in return."

The 7th Law is the

LAW of GENDER

Gender is in everything,
everything has it's masculine and feminine principles.
Gender manifests on all planes.

This Law is easier to explain
as we know that both male & females exist in both humans and animals.
But this masculine & feminine energy also exists in
plants, electrons, magnetic poles
and in the creative nature of all things on all planes.

Within every woman lies all the latent qualities of a man
and within every man those of a woman.
Nothing can come into being without the use of both of these energies.

The masculine contains a conquering assertive,
explorative and future driven energy.
Whereas, the feminine contains a receptive,
nourishing, protective and present energy.

These energies balance each other.

Gender is responsible for creation, generation and regeneration.

By examining our own lives
and determining how balanced we are with each of these energies,
we can adjust ourselves accordingly
to create our desires in a more effortless way,
when we balance the two.

.

To have complete control over your life,
you must master your own existence.
Set the intention that you will,
'Master' each of these Laws, one by one,
in order to manifest a life of true freedom.

.

Now you know the Laws...
let us P'RAISE unConditional Love...

First...how did I come into this knowledge?

I was in the shower *(how is it that most of the greatest ideas, are when we get in the shower?)*
...and holding the bottle of conditioner for my hair,
and I remembered un'CONDITION'al LOVE...
a LOVE without CONDITIONs

How would that FEEL?
Fantastic!

...So, what are CONDITIONS?

Well, my hair is tangled *(a Condition)*,
and this stuff gets out the tangles *(unConditions the condition)*.

But I had to think, why is my hair tangled?
...get to the root *(haha)* of the question and you get all the answers.

So my hair is tangled due to the wind, sleeping, hairspray etc...
All things that are outside of myself.
And so I use a product that is outside of me,
to unCondition a Condition that is outside of me.

And so, how does it FEEL when I have used the CONDITIONER?
Fantastic!

So, what if my sickness *(which is a Condition)* can be untangled?.
(and we all know there are many bottles of sickness unConditioner out there).

I had to keep asking myself, to get to the root of the problem.
.
.
.
*So, why was I sick on the inside?

"The mind acts as an enemy for those who don't control it."
Bhagavad Gita

.

.

"The distinction between past, present and future is only a stubbornly persistent illusion." Albert Einstein

.

.

"In our universe we are tuned into the frequency that corresponds to physical reality. But there are an infinite number of parallel realities coexisting with us in the same room, although we cannot tune into them." Steven Weinberg (Nobel Prize Quantum Physicist)
(I question this reply, as some can!)

.

.

*So, how can I make my Condition better NOW!...?

.

.

"A wise man, recognizing that the world is but an illusion, does not act as if it is real, so (therefore) he escapes the suffering." Buddha

.

.

*...and that is helpful!!???

Maybe not at this moment but keep reading....
because after Buddha, in good time and understanding,
even Abraham Lincoln said,
"To believe in the things you can see and touch is no belief at all: but to believe in the unseen is a triumph and a blessing."

.

.

*So, what is unCONDITIONAL Love?

It is a part of a Law...the Law of Polarity.

Just as there is a Law of Gravity,
and you know that Gravity works whether you want it to or not,
although you can try to tame it and work with it,
Gravity will always be Gravity, and it will always be there.
It is Immutable.

Love is always there.
Love is also Immutable.
Love is the only power for good.
There is only the one power for good, all the others are the
emotions you feel on your way up to the one power for good.

And that is what you are here to do...be good.

"This is an eternal and fundamental principle, inherent in all things, in every system of philosophy, in every religion and in every science. There is no getting away from the Law of Love." Charles Haanel

"Let our lives be good, and the times are good. We make our times; such as we are, such are the times." St Augustine

*So, why is it unConditional Love?

Firstly, what is your Condition?

What is the first thing that comes to mind when you are asked,
'How are you?'
or 'What are you?'
or 'Who are you?'
or 'Where are you?'

...that is your Condition.

Everything you are believing about yourself is a Condition....so you can be in any experience that you label yourself to be such as...
a Teacher, Builder, healthy, sick, cold, fat, tall, happy, married, kind, male, female (although you can now change that Condition too!) lonely, angry, employed, at home, on holiday, all Conditions are experiences.

...and does it FEEL good?

"Feeling is the secret." Neville Goddard

Are you happy in your Condition?

Are you stuck in your Condition?

Are you wanting to stay in your Condition of.......

PEACE
JOY
LOVE
APPRECIATION
HAPPINESS
BELIEF
OPTIMISM
HOPE
CONTENTMENT
courage
pride
boredom
pessimism
frustration
worry
blame
anger
jealousy
fear
grief
despair
guilt
shame

As you can see, we rise from the lower emotions,
up into the feelings of Goodness, Happiness and Peace.
.

.
*"You are rewarded not according to your work or your time,
but according to the measure of your Love."* St Catherine of Siena

Now, when you are thinking about your Condition,
you are not thinking about Love are you?

...unless you are actually in Love!

A Condition is a Condition of anything, other than Love.
A set of beliefs that you have collected together and formed into an
experience, that you are now experiencing.

You created it...how fantastic is that!
.

*I did not create my experience!!

What do you mean you did not create it?
You are arguing with a Condition that you are experiencing,
that you have chosen to experience?
.

*"The emotions must be called upon to give feeling to the thought so it
will take form."* Charles Haanel
.

.

*I certainly did not choose this experience!
.

What do you mean you did not choose it?
Just like Gravity, every experience is with you because you have
chosen it,

Isn't that fantastic?
.

*No
.

Why are you not enjoying your Condition?
Are you in pain?
Are you in lack?
Are you alone?
Are you happy?
Are you working?...................................
Are you not wanting to work?
.

.

"Poverty consists in feeling poor." Ralph Waldo Emerson
.

"Certainly, knowledge is a lock and its key is the question." Jafar al Sadiq
.
.

Every answer is given in reply to a question.

"Why are you not enjoying your Condition?"...
is a judgement upon the Condition.
The Condition you are experiencing now,
the one that you have chosen!

Now, there may be a few of you who are actually enjoying your
Condition now....

You have plenty of money in the bank.
You are in good health.
You have loads of friends.
You have a job you enjoy, or a job that you created and it is running
well and successfully.
You have a wife and family that you love.
You are enjoying this talk (haha).

And so you have Mastered the Condition of Mind...
Keep up the good work.
Well done.
.
.

*"When you realize there is nothing lacking, the whole world belongs to
you."* Lao Tzu
.
.

So, to the few here who are seeking answers as to why they are
not enjoying their Condition.
.
.

*"Be careful of your moods and feelings,
for there is an unbroken connection between your feelings and your
visible world."* Neville Goddard
.
.

Here
is
the
Answer...

LOVE .

"Knowing that you have working with you a force, which never yet has failed in anything it has undertaken, you can go ahead in the confident knowledge that it will not fail in your case either." Robert Collier

.

.

Yes, that really is all you need!

Because...

IT IS A LAW

Just as Gravity is a Law.

There is a Law of Love that works whether you want it to or not.
It is always there, and keeps on Loving, even if we don't!

It is also in partnership with Law of Vibration (Immutable) and the Law of Attraction (Mutable) and those Laws bring you everything that you THINK about.

*Oh dear!

Yes, EVERYTHING YOU THINK ABOUT,
SPEAK ABOUT, WRITE ABOUT....

*Oh dear!

...are you now understanding why you are in the Condition you are in?

*How will I understand the Law of Love?

Now you are asking the right question...well done.
To get a question answered correctly,
and so that you can understand the answer,
you need LOVE!

*Whaaaat?
I need the answer, not Love!

.

If you just want the answer, an answer will be given to you,
an answer will always be given to you
...but you may not be able to understand it !

Unless it is at the same level of Mind that you are in at this time...
(and that is the low level of questioning mind!)

And it may not help you change the Condition that you are wishing to free yourself from at this time
...because you do not understand the healing/inspirational answer from a higher level!

Albert Einstein taught us about the differing levels of Mind and solutions...
"We cannot solve our problems with the same thinking we used, when we created them."

.

.

*How will I understand it?

By Loving.

*How do I understand the answer you have just given me now? I do not understand how Loving can get me out of a Condition that I am experiencing now!

.

"Everything is possible to those who believe." Jesus Christ (Mark 9:23)

.

.

You do not know why you must Love to change a Condition,
...is that correct?

*Yes

Please state what you think (and it is only what YOU think) your Condition is at this time.

*I am depressed.

.

.

"Capture the feeling associated with your realized wish, by assuming the feeling that would be yours were you already in possession of the thing you desire, and your wish will objectify itself." Neville Goddard

.

.

.

Do you understand the Law of Gravity?

*I think so, if I drop something it will always land on the floor, it will not go up into the sky.

And you now agree that there is a Law of Gravity.

*Yes

Now, I have previously informed you that there is a Law of Mentalism...did you know there is a Law of Mentalism?

*No, I did not

Are you interested in understanding the Law of Mentalism further?

*Will it help me out of my Condition?

It will help you understand your Condition, and it will take you time to understand why you are in your Condition... but it appears that you are in a hurry to remove yourself from your Condition at this time...is that correct?

*Yes

But you do understand that there is a Law of Mentalism, and it is always with us, and it is there whether we know how to use it correctly or not, and it is Immutable, meaning it doesn't change... is that correct?

*Yes

And now you know that there is a Law of Mentalism, you understand that you can return to learn more about it after, you have released yourself from the Condition that you do not want to experience any further...is that correct?

*Yes

And let us remind ourselves of the Condition that you are finding yourself uncomfortable in at this time, please...

*I am depressed.

Who do you Love?

*I love my sons

How do you FEEL when you THINK about your sons?
...and understand that it is a Law of Mentalism, and that it delivers
everything that you focus upon and feel when you are Thinking.

*personal reply

.
.

"Hatred paralyses life; Love releases it.
Hatred confuses life; Love harmonizes it.
Hatred darkens life; Love illuminates it." Martin Luther King Jr

.

.

Really...even though you love your sons you feel sad?
How can that be?
Love is a feeling that feels good and positive. And so you are not in
a Loving feeling with your sons, you are in sadness when you think
about your sons...is that correct?

*Yes

So we can truthfully say, you are sad when you think about your
sons, even though you say that you love them...is that correct?

*Yes.....So how can I change that Condition?

We use unConditional Love!
You have a Condition that is NOT Love when you think about your
sons, so we have to now unCondition your thinking about your
sons...shall we do that?

.

.

"When ever anyone has offended me, I try to raise my soul so high that
the offence cannot reach it." Rene Descartes

.

.

*Yes please

Why are you sad when you think about your sons?

*personal reply

So it is not really about your sons, it is the situation around your sons, from the past that is in your thoughts. You keep remembering the past experience, the past Condition and that is tainting your Love for your sons at this time...is that correct?

*Yes, I can see that now

And so without the Condition of (personal Condition), how do you see your sons now?

*They are just 2 boys, grown men now, who have chosen where they want to be, and it is always their choice to think what they want about me. And seeing as I wasn't there much in their past, it is understandable.

So, there is a Law of Mentalism, and it is available to everyone, and if they think about you and focus upon you, then they Love you?

*Yes

Really...so all thoughts are good thoughts???
.
.
"Your own soul is nourished when you are kind; it is destroyed when you are cruel." King Solomon in Proverbs 11:17
.
.
*No............Oh dear, I understand now

Well done...are you ok?

*Yes

Shall we return to the Condition that you wish to release yourself from?

*No...I am in a different Condition now

Yes you are, and how does that feel?

*Not very good at all!
.
.

*"If a man speaks or acts with an evil thought, pain follows him.
If a man speaks or acts with a pure thought, happiness follows him,
like a shadow that never leaves him."* Buddha

.

.

So, let us get back to learning about the Law of Love shall we?

*Yes please

.

.

*"Taking the 1st step with a good thought,
the 2nd with a good word,
and the 3rd with a good deed,
I entered Paradise."* Book of Arda Viraf

.

.

OK, time for a cup of tea,
and then I can explain more with some tea.

.

"Happiness depends upon ourselves." Aristotle

.

.

*Yes, that sounds like a very good idea.

Yes, you heard me correctly, and it is a very good idea, your
hearing sense is working correctly, and soon you will be using your
taste sense, that will experience my great idea that came from
within me, as an act of Love to make you, and I, FEEL better.

The thought started from within, I spoke what I thought, and you
heard the idea, and now we shall experience that idea in china
teacups. I have changed a Condition of one without tea, to a
Condition with tea.
Will it change the Love Condition?

***I don't know, although a cup of tea usually makes me feel
better in any Condition.**

Let me make the tea and let's discuss it further.
And shall we have some lunch too?

*That depends on what you have, I don't eat meat anymore

.

Now we are entering a huge pot of options and different paths of discussion over the simple question of lunch.
Shall we keep things simple and just have tea?

* Have you any biscuits?

Yes I do, and they are perfect with tea.
.
.
"Keep your mind as much as you can from dwelling on your ailment.
Think of strength and power and you will draw it to you.
Think of good health and you will get it." Prentice Mulford
.

Now, thinking about tea and lunch is keeping us from Love.
Do you understand?
.
.
"It's not how much we give but how much Love we put into giving."
Mother Teresa
.

*I thought thinking about Love, got me into the FEELING of Love...

YES!!! You have got it correct, well done.
All that talk of tea and your sons and (personal Condition) and lunch and decisions is not LOVE is it?

They are all Conditions **OUT** of LOVE.

We have to unCondition the Condition, to bring us back into Love, to change the Condition...you see?

*Not when you put it that way, no I don't.

Well, you tell me how you get into the FEELING of Love...
.
.
"If you require Love, try to realize that the only way to get Love is by giving it, that the more you give the more you will get, and the only way you can give it is to fill yourself up with it, until you become a magnet, and so then you attract more Love." Charles Haanel
.
.

*I sit and think about all the things I love to do that makes me feel good, all the people I love that make me feel good, and it seems that is not my sons at this time...

Only because you have to push out the thoughts of the past hurts with thoughts of Love now, to bring back the feeling of Love about your sons.
When you think so much about what you do Love,
you cannot think about what you do not Love,
as we can only think one thought at a time!

*...but that sounds like I don't love my sons?

At this time that appears to be correct, as you have some past issues that still cloud the thought of your sons, with the past thoughts...that are not actually correct now.

*Why aren't they correct now?
They still are... (personal reply)

And you are still thinking thoughts that do not feel good, rather than ones that make you feel good and can actually change the Condition.

.
.

"All you can possibly need or desire is already yours. Call your desires into being by imagining and feeling your wish fulfilled." Neville Goddard
.

.
*How?

I thought you would never ask!
But you did touch on it just a few moments ago, by saying you had to think thoughts of Love to feel Love.

*Yes I did, but it didn't last long did it.

Without practice it never does.   It is very easy to slip back into the past thoughts of judgement and remembering past hurts that cloud a feeling of Love now...but with every good feeling thought, to cover every bad thought, it all takes practice.
.
.

"A man who is master of himself can end a sorrow as he can invent a pleasure. I don't want to be at the mercy of my emotions. I want to use them, to enjoy them and to dominate them." Oscar Wilde

*We practice bad things?

If we keep focusing upon them and having thoughts about them, we slip back into bad thoughts and keep creating them because one bad thought creates another.
We have a momentum of bad thoughts and so it takes some effort to turn a momentum of bad thoughts into a stream of good thought momentum.
It is all part of the Law of Polarity and the Law of Attraction, and they are part of the Principle Law of Love.

"Extend to each person, no matter how trivial the contact, all the care and kindness and understanding and Love that you can muster, and do it with no thought of any reward. Your life will never be the same again."
Og Mandino

see this **A**?

*Yes

Well, you can see that there is a triangle in the middle of it, that is surrounded, yes?

*Yes

And let us just say that there is a flow of bad thoughts rising from below the 'A'....
They can actually get into a small part of the 'A' and some stay there, but as the flow is always flowing, they keep moving into that space and are pushed out and up and around the 'A' and keep flowing onwards and upwards.
And there is still the section that is protected from all the bad thoughts...right?

*Right

So if there are bad thoughts flowing upwards, and all around the 'A' what do you think is inside of the triangle in the middle?

*Good thoughts?

Correct, and if you were trapped in a small cell with no escape, how would you feel?

*Bad

No, because you are IN good thoughts!
And good thoughts stay good thoughts, no matter what is happening on the outside of them.

Even if all that they see and hear, taste and smell is bad, they still FEEL GOOD because they are good thoughts...and Good thoughts are thoughts of Love.

So, what you hear, smell, taste and see are all 'Senses' of what is outside of you.
Yet inside of you, is the real FEELING of Goodness and Love.
It is not outside of you...it is always in you, until...

*...Until..?

Until you turn the 'A' (which is only an example for this purpose) around...and as my typewriter does not have an upside down 'A' you will have to draw one yourself.
Please do that now...

* OK

Excellent

Now, remember that the bad thoughts are flowing from the bottom of the page upwards,

*Just like a plant does

That is correct.

Bad thoughts are weed thoughts,
and too many weed thoughts can overcome good thought seeds.
Seeds of bad thoughts are growing upwards,
just as seeds of good thoughts also grow upwards.

It is just up to YOU to CHOOSE which seeds to plant.
.
.
"Muddy water, let stand, becomes clear." Lao Tzu
.
.
*How do I do that?

Well, you are sifting through all sorts of Thoughts.
Good, bad, past, present, and thoughts you hope for in the future.
Correct and mistaken perceptions, imagination and memories.

Because there is a Law of Mentalism that is always with us, and is
there to be used whenever we want to, whether we know how to
use it correctly or not.

*So how do I get to think the good thoughts?

By sitting STILL in Meditation, SMILING and LISTENING.

The answer will come at differing levels of your giving,
and feeling Love.
The more Love you feel, the higher the level of Solution to your
Condition.
And acceptance (receiving) of the answer, is the feeling of
wonderful inspiration...you just know it is right.
That woooowhoooooo feeling!

So keep smiling and feeling Love in that Smile.

But when you stop asking questions,
you no longer enter the state of Thought,
or you get lazy and stop accepting the Solutions of Thought.

Maybe you do not agree with Thought,
and thus place yourself in a state of non-Thought.

Your Doctors call it dementia.

We have helped you to try to understand easier, it by giving it the word 'demen', because a 'demon' reminds you of a negative entity, ...that does not exist ....unless you think it does...!

And as you now know, there is a Law of Thinking that works in harmony with the other Laws to bring you what you think about (whether you know how it works or not), just like Gravity and Love.

*I really need to know more about that later... but you say that dementia is bad thoughts?
.

.

"Nothing is either good or bad, but thinking makes it so."
William Shakespeare
.

.

It starts that way,
and the cells have to shut the brain down so that it can not harm the body with its negative thoughts.

The body is under your control and obeys your thoughts and word orders, *(the Law of Mentalism).*
When you keep thinking of sickness and speaking about your illnesses, you create more of the same, *(the Law of Vibration).*
And so the cells then have to 'mutiny' to save the body, *(the Law of Sacrifice).*
The cells know exactly what to do to keep healthy *(the Law of Success).*
Yet they always obey their Captain, *(the Law of Obedience).*

And seeing as YOU are the Captain, you tell/think what the cells should be or do.
And too many thoughts of sickness is against the good programming of the cells, and so they start a 'mutiny' to protect themselves *(the Law of Sacrifice).*

They have to.....to stay alive! *(the Law of Love).*

Remember, the cells are programmed to stay healthy to keep the 'Good' that is trapped in the 'A' safe.

It is the ultimate power pack for Good health.

Yet the Captain (YOU), is going crazy saying, he/she has this disease, that pain, this Condition, that Condition *(the Law of Mentalism)*...and the cells finally have enough and say,

"That's it, we have had enough, we canny take any more Captain." (I use the words of Scotty of the U.S.S. Enterprise in Star Trek, to help you understand better).

And so the cells shut the brain down so that no more thoughts (good or bad) can be thought.
And now the body of the ship is protected from the crazy Captain (YOU).

But sometimes there is so much damage, and so many negative cells, that the whole system is overloaded and the good keeps being overcome by the bad/negative cells, and the body deteriorates to death *(the Law of Mentalism & the Law of Correspondence)*.

.
.

"There is nothing in biology yet found that indicates the inevitability of death. This suggests to me that it is not at all inevitable and that it is only a matter of time before biologists discover what it is that is causing us the trouble." Richard Feynman (Nobel Quantum Physicist)

.
.

So the cells do need the Captain (YOU) to get your act together to LOVE them back to good health again..... *(the Law of Rhythm)*
YOU (Captain) and the cells, need each other to survive!

It is true, you do have a Condition,
brought on by thoughts of fear of the Condition.
Yet as you have not been taught to unCondition this Condition,
you remain in Condition...ok?

*Whaat?...so my Dad brought on his own dementia?

.
.

"For as he thinketh in his heart, so is he." King Solomon (Proverbs 23:7)

.
.
.

"If we will be quiet and ready enough, we shall find compensation in every disappointment." Henry David Thoreau

.
.

Yes, by not knowing he has to control his Thoughts and to think more and feel more in LOVE.
No one told him how to do this.

And so his cells shut his brain down so he could stay physically on the planet, until a Solution could be found to this question of dementia.

That is what all good cells do...
they unCondition the Condition of dementia, because they LOVE the body so much..
Bad cells create more of the same, and rot the body from the inside out.

There are good cells and bad cells,
created by the Thoughts of good and bad...
.

.
"For the thing that I fear comes upon me, and what I dread befalls me."
Job 3:25
.

But there is also a way to turn a bad cell into a good cell...
with FEELINGS of LOVE !

And if you do not LOVE,
your bad cells overcome the good
and cause disease in the good cells.

When you LOVE,
you create more good cells which overcome the bad cells.

And you can only do this with
THOUGHTS & FEELINGS of LOVE.
More feelings of Love create more good cells.

More bad 'feelings' create more bad cells.

Can I make this explanation any simpler for you to understand?
.

.
"Your emotions affect every cell in your body.
Mind and body, mental and physical, are intertwined." Thomas Tutko

*No...I understand.

"If you are distressed by anything external, the pain is not due to the thing itself, but to your estimate of it; and this you have the power to revoke at any moment." Marcus Aurelius

"The power is from within, we cannot receive it unless we give it." Charles Haanel

Are you ok?

"Remember, there is no such thing as a small act of kindness. Every act creates a ripple with no logical end." Scott Adams

* I need a moment to take this in.

We know you don't feel good at this time knowing this?
Due to your past levels of processing information, you have found yourself confused, as it doesn't equate to past methods of healing that you have learnt before.
We have overloaded you full of good information, into a mind that is not equipped to process it yet.

But when you have acknowledged the information fully, you will be so thankful and so Loving!

"Natural forces within us are the true healers of disease." Hippocrates (Father of Western Medicine)

*No, ...I don't feel good at the moment.

And now you will learn to unCondition the low feeling you feel at this time, because you have learnt this information.
If you stay in the low feeling it will create more of the same.
You know that now don't you?

*Yes, I know that now, but I don't know how to turn it around, I feel so numb by that information.

It is imperative that you unCondition this low feeling now!!!!

*How, I really don't want to...but I am shocked by it

.

.

"Face towards the perfect image of every organ, and the shadows of disease will never touch you."   Robert Collier

.

.

What do you LOVE?
not Who,
but
What do you LOVE?

.

.

.

.

.

* I love sweets

Why?

*Because they are sweet, and I don't know why, they just taste good and even though I am told I shouldn't eat them, I love sweets.

We wont trouble ourselves as to why you think you shouldn't eat them now, so...what else do you LOVE?

*Kittens and cats

.

"The Law of Love could be best understood and learned through little children." Mahatma Gandhi

.

.

And...is there any part of your body that you really Love??

*Fluffy jumpers, baggy trousers, my sofa, my blanket, my house, my car...I love my car...I love my house, I love my phone, I love my computer, I love my books, I love my body, I love my body, Yes, actually I really do love my body......

Well done, you started to speak of Love, not just listing the things you Love, you started to use the word 'Love' and then what you Love, well done.

SPEAKING of Love creates more thoughts of what you Love, and thoughts and WORDS of Love create feelings of Love, and FEELINGS of Love creates more Love, and more LOVE creates the good cells that keep you healthy ...so keep going...
What do you LOVE?

* I love gardening, I love taking cuttings and growing new plants, I love walking and kayaking and I love swimming in the sea whatever the weather, I love being at home, I love helping people, I love my sons...

Well done....
.
.
"As your faith is strengthened you will find that there is no longer the need to have a sense of control, that things will flow as they will, and that you will flow with them, to your great delight and benefit."
Wingate Paine
.
.
*I love my ex-husband but not in that way, I love him because I used to love him, and it feels better to love him than not to love him...he can love who he wants to now, and I love myself for loving everyone, I love how I have overcome many difficulties and I love how I still love...and I LOVE this FEELING I now feel in my tummy, that feels good and it feels like love...so I love that, and I feel better now, and I thank you for pulling me away from those numb thoughts from that dementia information you gave me....I will look at it again later when I feel I can handle the information better....I understand now that I have to have more good feeling thoughts than bad ones, and I love the way it feels to know that now...that is liberating....and is it freedom?

"Gratitude is a vaccine, an antitoxin and an antiseptic." John Henry Jowett

"Hate is not conquered by hate.
Hate is conquered by Love.
This is a Law eternal." Buddha

Yes it is freedom when you can turn away from a low Condition and raise yourself up into a higher Condition.

That is unConditional Love,
and it is the best work you can do for yourself at this time.

And when you feel even better you can go back to work.
You will know when that is, because you will feel uncomfortable (see another unCondition!).

How to turn unComfortable in Comfortable?
FEEL the Loving thoughts of Comfort.

And if you can keep good thoughts going throughout 51% of your day, you have tipped the scale for good health going your way. Make it 75% and you really are keeping on top of your good health...ok!

I know you don't like me to speak about Jesus much, but He did say something really useful.
Well, He said a lot of useful things, and now we know why...
but this is what will fit in here very well...

"Give, and it will be given to you...for by your standard of measure it will be measured to you in return." as stated in Luke 6:38

So, GIVE positivity and your RECEIVE back positivity; GIVE negativity and your RECEIVE back negativity.
Whatever you give out in life, must return to you.
It is the physics and mathematics of the universe.

And Jesus got His information from the same cloud that Sophocles the Greek Playwright also visited...

"One word frees us of all the weight and pain of life. That word is Love."
...and that was nearly 500 years before the Bible was written.

Here's another quote that fits here well...
"To every action, there is an equal and opposite reaction." Isaac Newton

and he was around in the 1700s ...and some understand his writings better than that of Jesus, yet it is the same theory, just said at different times, in a different way, that others of that generation would understand.

Every action of GIVING creates an opposite action of RECEIVING and what you RECEIVE is always equal to what you have GIVEN.

...and just because others don't return Love to you, remember...
.

.

"Whether humanity will consciously follow the Law of Love, I do not know. But that need not disturb me. The Law will work just as the Law of Gravitation works, whether we accept it or not." Mahatma Gandhi (and he was around in the 1900s).

.

.

...and back to Jesus again...
"Then you will know the truth and the Truth will set you free." John 8:32
.

.

So be Grateful for everything you have received in your life (past),
and everything you are receiving in your life (present),
and for everything you want in your life (future),
as though you have received it already.

And one last one...
"Love is the fulfilling of the Law" St Paul 13:10.....Thank you.
.

.

What that means is...

All the Laws are covered, when you LOVE...
The Law of Thinking & Supply & Attraction & Receiving & Increase & Compensation & Non-Resistance & Forgiveness & Sacrifice & Obedience and Success !

"Gratitude for the abundance you have received, is the best insurance that the abundance will continue." Muhammad

.

.

And that really FEELS GOOD doesn't it...well done.
Is there anything you wish to add?

*Have we spelt 'Lord' incorrectly?
Is it meant to be Lawd ?
The bringer of the Laws of Love!

Well, the Word 'Lord' is a whole sentence in itself.

We use it to remind ourselves...
Love **or d**eath

And the Word 'Law'd' reminds us...
While we are here to keep the **Law,** there is always **d**eath.
But it is your CHOICE how quickly you want to leave this planet,
by breaking the Laws of Good Health and LOVE.

It is all up to YOU...
Captain!

*Thank you!

Yes, that FEELS GOOD too...Thank you.!

.

.

"You cannot exercise much power without gratitude, because it is gratitude that keeps you connected with power." Wallace Wattles

.

.

*Oh, what about the upside down 'A' ?

Yes, the unConditioned 'A' ....glad you remembered, well done...well it lived 'Happily ever after'.

*Now you are being silly

Yes, I am...
Can you tell me what happens to the upside down 'A' please?

*Well, if we opened the door to the triangle cell when it was right side up, 'A' all the goodness would fall out and there would be none left for the rest of our journey.
And now it is the other way up, we don't have to open the door at all, and the goodness can be planted seed by seed at the bottom of the page, to grow into the stream of Good Thoughts. And as they grow upwards, they can flow easily past the upside down 'A'...

But won't it run out of Good seeds to plant?

*We can open the door and refill it when we need to, with other good thought seeds, and keep the door shut to any bad thought weed seeds, that may have been planted by someone else...and maybe growing nearby.

Don't forget to 'Love thy neighbour as thy self'.
As that is a Golden rule that creates Good seeds.
.
.
"The entire Law is summed up in a single command, Love your neighbour as yourself." St Paul in Galatians 5:14
.
.
*LOVE IS the rule
...and Love creates more of itself by the Law of Attraction!

You really are getting the hang of this now....well done indeed!

*Thank you
.
.
"If the only prayer you say in your entire life is - 'Thank you' - that is enough." Meister Eckhart
.
.
"You have no cause for anything but gratitude and joy." Buddha
.
.
"When the heart is set right, then the personal life is cultivated. When the personal life is cultivated, the home life is regulated. When the home life is regulated, then the national life is orderly. And when the national life is orderly, then the world is at peace."
Confucius.

Opening your chakras

To gain control of your Emotions,
you must gain balance within yourself
before
you can bring balance to your world.

In order to Master the Emotions,
you must open all the chakras.

Here are the basics.......

.

.

.

Water flows through a stream,
much like Energy flows through your body.
A stream can create pools that flow slower
than the main stream,
and these pools are like our chakra's.

Chakra's are pools of spiralling energy
in our bodies....
And if nothing else was around,
these pools would flow pure and clear.
However, life is messy
and things tend to fall into the stream...

....and then what happens?

...the stream cannot flow
when there is a blockage...!

But, if we open the paths
between the pools,
the energy flows.

.

.

.

There are 7 Chakra's that go UP the body.

Each pool of Energy has a purpose
and can be blocked by a specific kind
of emotional muck.

.

.

.

BE WARNED!

OPENING THE CHAKRA'S
IS AN INTENSE EXPERIENCE,

& ONCE YOU BEGIN THE PROCESS,
YOU CANNOT STOP
UNTIL ALL 7 ARE OPEN

Are you ready?
?
?

.
.
.
.
.

STEP ONE
...Let your fears flow down stream...

First we will clear the Earth Chakra
located at the base of the spine,
it deals with survival
and is blocked by fear.

What are you most afraid of....?

Let your fears become clear...

.
.
.
.
.
.
.
.
.

Your vision is not real
you are concerned for your survival

...but you must surrender those fears,

let your fears flow down the stream.

.
.
.
.
.
.

STEP TWO

...release all blame and guilt within you...

This is the Water Chakra,
located in the area of the sexual organs.

This Chakra deals with pleasure,
and is blocked by guilt.

Now, look at all the guilt
which burdens you so...

What do you blame yourself for.....?

.
.
.
.
.

.

.

.

.

.

.

.

Accept the reality
that these things happen...!

...but do not let them cloud
and poison your energy.

If you are to be
a positive influence on the world,
you need to

FORGIVE YOURSELF!

.

.

.

.

.

.

.

.

.

.

.

.

STEP THREE

...Accept and Love all aspects of who you are
...even your mistakes!

This is the Fire Chakra,
and is located in the stomach.

This Chakra deals with Will Power and is
blocked by shame.

What are you ashamed of.....?

What are your biggest disappointments
in your self...?

.

.

.

.

.

.

.

.

.

.

.

.

.

.

You will never find balance
if you deny this part of your life.

You are who you are,
and so you learn to control
and enjoy your Will Power.

.

.

.

.

.

.

.

.

.

.

.

.

.

.

.

STEP FOUR

...release all your sadness and loss...

The 4th chakra is located in the Heart,
it deals with Love,
and is blocked by grief.

Lay all your grief out in front of you....

.

.

.

.

.

.

.

.

.

.

.

.

.

You have indeed felt a great loss,

...but Love is a form of Energy
and it swirls all around us.

Those who loved you,
their Love has not left this world,

it is still inside of your heart,
and is reborn
in the form of new Love.

.

.

Let the pain flow away...

.

.

.

very good

.

.

.

.
.
.
.

STEP FIVE

release your denial & the lies you tell yourself

The 5th chakra is the Sound chakra,
located in the throat,
it deals with the Truth
and is blocked by lies
(the ones we tell ourselves)

You cannot lie about your own nature,
you must accept that
you are who you are!

Who are you?

What feels good being who you really are?

.
.
.
.

.

.

.

.

.

Who do you really want to be?.

Then that is you...!

Now, you have opened your Truth
of who you really are..!

So, that feels good doesn't it ?

And only you lie to yourself...!

Better...?

.

.

.

.

.

Good

.

.

.

STEP SIX
...release all illusions within yourself...

The 6th pool of Energy is the Light chakra,
and is located in the centre of the forehead.
This chakra deals with insight
and is blocked by illusion.

The greatest illusion of this world
is the illusion of separation.
Things you think that are separate
and different
are actually one and the same!

Just like each individual country of the world.
We are all one people,
but we live as if we are divided.

We are all connected.

Even the separation of the 4 elements
is an illusion.

If you open your mind
you will see all the elements are one...
4 parts of the same whole,
even metal is just a part of Earth
that has been purified and refined.

We are one and the same

.

.

.

.

STEP SEVEN

...release all your earthly attachments,
let go of all you have grown to love...

The Thought chakra is located
at the crown of the head,
it deals with Pure Cosmic Energy
and is blocked by earthly attachment.

Once you open this chakra
you will be able to go in and out
of the Emotional state at will,
and when you are in an Emotion,
you will have complete control
and awareness
of all of your actions.

Meditate,
on what attaches you to this world...?

.

.

.

.

.

.

.

Now, let all those attachments go,
let them flow down the river,
forgotten.

Learn to let go of the one's you love,
or you cannot let the
Pure Cosmic Energy
flow in from the Universe.

You must learn to let go.

To Master the Emotional state
you must open all the chakras.

Surrender yourself.

Now, think of your attachments,
and let them go...

.

.

.

Let the Pure Cosmic Energy flow...

You are then able to connect
to your perfect or higher self
who knows your path...

Your destiny
Your joys
Your loves
Your peace
Your prosperity.

When you have surrendered
and let your fears go,
you will have cleared your Earth Chakra,
and it will bring you more happiness
and good thoughts.

A blocked Earth Chakra is when
you are fearful and you are worried,
this must be cleared regularly.

You FEEL worried,
so you know your Earth Chakra is blocked.

When you feel happy and carefree,
you know you have a clear flow
and your Earth Chakra
is working correctly.

This process becomes easier
the more you understand it,
and know how to clear yourself
when you become worried.

Worry will become less
the more you clear,
and the more you clear
the less you worry!

Remember...
what you clear from one pool
will flow into the next...
that is why these fears keep surfacing,
because they become trapped
in the next pool.

So, you clear, in order to clear in order!

I tell my clients to SMILE...

just SMILE...

Now, how does that feel?

And so you keep SMILING until you feel a little better...
and then a bigger better...
and then you FEEL GOOD.

The actual task of SMILING removes the brain and questioning,
and subtly introduces themselves to their god self....and their god
self is always Happiness and Calm....and Peace

....and that does FEEL GOOD.

And then when they FEEL GOOD,
they can then ask their self the questions,
if that is what they want!

They may want to ask a different question...
and that is their choice as they are in communication with self...
and that is actually private!

So when you have guided them...
then leave them to chat happily with their self,
to get the answers they need to hear to bring them a better life.

Get the brain out of the room...
out of the way...
and allow them to converse in Truth and Peace.

Oh, and when you enter the room again...
The FEELING IS FANTASTIC.....BLESSED!

Peace be with you

Yogi Sally Ann Slight

YSAS REPLY>>>>>>>it will take time for you to believe words,
it is easier for you to believe from experience.

Your thoughts and feelings created this health issue,
they were of lower emotions and feelings,
and only you know what you have thought throughout your life time.

And what you are experiencing now is from your thoughts and
beliefs about disease and bad health.

The only way to find relief from bad health,
is to find the good health that is actual still in you,

it has been forgotten by your attention on the bad health.

So, what part of you is in good health?

Focus on that part,
be thankful for the good health you do have,

in any part of you that is in good health.

That is the only thing you focus on now,
from this moment,
that is the whole of you.

That feeling of thanks for this part of good health will create more
good cells,
for they are now being paid attention to.
They are the focus for your every thought,
every feeling,
every word.

When anyone asks you, "How you are now?"
you can say,
"I am in good health."

Because that is where your focus is now,
IN good health.

All other thoughts have passed from this moment.

You are turning your thoughts around.
You are turning your mind around from bad to good.

and only you can do this for yourself.

So you 'HAVE' learnt from experience,
you have experienced the bad,
you are an expert in bad health.

Now turn that thought around and focus on Kindness, Goodness,
Peace, Happiness, Joy, Comfort and Good Health.

Peace be with you child

Yogi Sally Ann Slight

.

.

.

.

YSAS REPLY>>>>>>>your feelings create your life.

So you experience all those things that your partner is delivering to
you, because that is what you think he is!

Can you start to Love him again?

Sit, be still and smile,
and feel that smile deep within you,
be thankful for all the good in your life now.

Do not judge yourself or another.

Just feel love and thanks for all the good in your life now.

Thankful for the eyes that read this.
For the book that brings you this message.
for the food in your cupboards.
The money in your bank.
The love in your heart.

Feel that thankfulness grow within you and you send that out into
the world.

Every time you feel low,
you have to bring yourself up to the level of love by working at it.

Just as you go to the gym to work your muscles,
you work on your Love in your heart and mind.

Sit, be still and smile...
and feel that goodness of every memory of goodness,
and you create more good thoughts to create more memories.

One thought at a time in your mind,
so make it a good one.
Smile and love.

Feel good

You will not know the outcome,
until you experience it,
by noticing the change in those you Love.

Peace be with you

Yogi Sally Ann Slight

.

.

.

YSAS REPLY>>>>>When Karate Martial Artists break blocks,
they focus on the other side of the block.

Their focus is so true to their task,
that they cannot harm themselves,
as they are already on the other side of the block.

You too my dear,
are on the other side of bad health.

You are already in good health...
You are there,

waiting for you to join You there.

You have to change your beliefs about pain and damage.!
your cells know what to do...
so let them!

And you get on with a nice new hobby like gardening or painting, something creative.

Focus on what you want, and by doing something that does not involve thinking or speaking about disease, then you can easily let it go.

It does not exist in your experience.

Pain has an opposite, and is a Mutable Law, so it can be changed by degrees of knowing you are in good health.

OK.

Peace be with you

Yogi Sally Ann Slight

'

'

YSAS REPLY>>>>>>Love does not have any lower thought emotions.

When you are in jealousy, you are not 'in love' my dear, you are in jealousy!

Return to loving thoughts and you will be 'in love' again!

All lower thought forms that feel bad, need to be raised back up to Love.

HOW DO YOU DO THAT?

By being thankful to her for being your girlfriend!
She is a gift for you to Love.
To learn of Love,
and to practice Love.

Love feels good,

jealousy does not,

.

So it is easy to know when to be thankful,
and choose a good feeling thought that will raise you back up into
Love again.

It is only your choice.
And your feelings keep you on track.

Nothing she does can change your mind,
when you are in Love.

You can blame no one but yourself for your thoughts.

Feel good and everything goes very well for you, both.

Peace

Yogi Sally Ann Slight

'Trauma' is nothing more than being 'stuck' in what you believe.

.

.

.

.

.

.

.

.

.

THE MAP OF ASCENSION

...so you know where you are

...how far you have come

...how far you may still have to go

...and you can choose which direction to head in!

Peace

Serenity

Joy

Respect

Love

Understanding

Forgiveness

Optimism

Trust

Courage

pride/indifference

anger/hate

desire/craving

fear/anxiety

grief/regret

apathy/despair

guilt/blame

shame/humiliation

Where are you now?

Where do you want to be?

A STUDY IN THE USE OF 'THE MAP OF ASCENSION'
(Map of Consciousness by Dr David Hawkins)

QUESTION....Have you ever felt depressed? What does it really mean?
.

.

YSAS REPLY....you are in a lower level of emotional experience...you have accepted a thought form that lowers your emotion and so you suffer....time to change your mind ....and it starts with a smile...be thankful...Peace be with you
.

.

(name withheld) REPLY...BS. This kind of trite response to depression is an insult to people who suffer from it. It also shows a complete lack of understanding and empathy on your part. People who are dealing with depression certainly don't need you trivializing their condition.
.

.

YSAS REPLY....hahahahaha.......replying certainly keeps me happy.

You know, getting out of depression is so simple, it makes you angry!

(It is the, 'Why didn't I know this before?' sort of anger).

I have been there too you know!!

And by no one telling me how to climb out of my depression pit, I remained in it for far too long, and harmed myself with drugs I did not need, and I lost my family and friends (who are all returning to me now, thankfully!)

And so now because I found a way out, I can show you how, and you can rise to the higher levels of Happiness sooner (the skill is in maintaining the higher levels, and I can teach you that too!).

I am so glad you are rising up the emotional scale from *depression* to *anger* my dear (name withheld).

Now smile...
that will change the thought form to *criticism* (which you did too!).

Then you may experience some *worry*,
(due to you thinking, "Maybe this is something that can help me?").

Then rising above that...

You may experience some *disappointment*... (only in yourself and your thoughts, but that is ok too, it is just lack of understanding at this time, read on).

Then up into *irritation*... (and yes, it seems I did that to you too, although it was your thoughts about my reply that irritated you!).

Then you go up into *boredom*...
(especially with me, as you did not reply).

You then go up into *Satisfaction*...
(are you *satisfied* with this reply?......the Rolling Stones said, "I can't get no *satisfaction*", perhaps they were not told how to either!).

Then you go up into *Hope*...
(where you may now realize that there is an easier way out of *depression*, as shown here, and you *Hope* it can help you too!) So, now you feel *Hopeful* this may be of help.

Then you go up into *Enthusiasm*...
(you may feel you want to tell others that you are starting to feel better, and maybe you too can get others out of feeling so sad, mad, bad etc!).

Into *Excitement*...
(wow, I feel she could be right, what is the next step?).

Then up into *Passion*...
(you really do want to have a better life by understanding new ways of improvement....and maintaining them!).

Up into *Joy*...
(phew! I really am feeling better, I have got to tell more people about this stuff that makes me feel so much better).

And up into *Gratitude*...
(where you could have gone to straight away!!!.... by saying, 'Thank you for you answer").

And up to *LOVE*...
....and if you can stay in LOVE, you can get through the whole day (so John Lennon was right, "All You Need is Love").

And that gets you into *PEACE*...
(with the whole world........and Me!).

It's ok you are forgiven, I get told what you said a lot.

It is just the level of understanding you are on at the moment you read the TRUTH...and the TRUTH sparked off your *anger*, which is a higher level than *depression*, *despair guilt, envy, hate* and *fear*...so it really is good!

And there you have it (name withheld), ...that is *Enlightenment*!

It also shows a complete understanding and empathy on my part towards you, by giving you a full and "FREE" reply to your *angry* words, which I am so glad you wrote, as my reply will help so many others too.

So well done to you for getting *angry*, and well done to me for giving more of my many years of study & hard work away for "FREE".

Thank you very much,
(See, I am in *Gratitude* mode now, and that always feels good).

Peace be with you child.
It really is simple when you 'allow' yourself to feel better, and follow the process of *Enlightenment*.

Yogi Sally Ann Slight

YSAS REPLY>>>>>I hope you have laughed off the feeling of frustration today.

REMEMBER, when you are experiencing a low emotion,
due to a negative thought,
and you are accepting that thought...
There is no way for the good thought and experience to get through to you,
because you can only accept and act on one thought at a time.

THE VERY IDEA THAT COULD SAVE YOUR LIFE, COULD BE HOVERING JUST OUTSIDE OF YOUR MIND....WAITING FOR YOU TO ACCEPT IT, THINK IT AND PUT IT INTO ACTION.

...and yet YOU choose to remain in the negative experience !

For as long as YOU feel you have been unjustly treated,
or YOU feel you may have a disease,
or YOU think you do not have enough,
or YOU think you are not worthy or good enough......etc.

You will remain in the same negative experience,
and cause more damage to your body and mind.

And the more hurt YOU cause yourself,
the more difficult it will be to heal you,
either scientifically or Spiritually!

YOU have blocked out the good thought,
the solution to your problem,
by remaining in the complaint mode,
or
by accepting and fearing what is happening in this moment!

Now you know you can chose your thoughts...

Yes ?

So you choose to believe that your future is Good Health,

before you even start the process of appointments etc.

"I CHOOSE...
GOOD THOUGHTS,
GOOD EMOTIONS,
GOOD HEALTH,
GOOD NEWS."

And then allow the Doctor to deal with the damage that you have created, from all YOUR past negative thoughts and emotions !

And in this way you remain calm,
knowing that your healthy future is protected,
by YOUR OWN CHOICE OF GOOD THOUGHTS.

You heal yourself quicker and remain happy.
So you do not cause any further hurt to your body or mind,
by accepting another negative thought, and emotion.

You will have then regained your own power over negative thoughts,
and are open to the solutions that offer themselves to you,
to bring you more good health,
more happiness and success in all that you choose as your goal.

Please ASK if you need more understanding.

Peace be with you.

Yogi Sally Ann Slight

.

.

.

.

.

.

.

HEAVENLY VIRTUES
& HOW TO GET HAPPY!

The first 3 are known as the Spiritual Virtues.

1. FAITH is belief in the right things (including the Virtues!).
2. HOPE is taking a positive future view, that good will prevail.
3. CHARITY or LOVE is concern for, and active helping of, others.

The last four are called the Chief or Natural Virtues.

4. FORTITUDE or DILIGENCE is never giving up.
5. JUSTICE or PATIENCE is being fair and equitable with others.
6. KINDNESS or PRUDENCE is care of and moderation with money.
7. TEMPERANCE is moderation of needed things and abstinence from things which are not needed.

So what?

1a. If you follow the Virtues, you will be seen as a good person who is to be trusted.

1b. If you assume and act as if others follow the Virtues, then they are more likely to do so.

(this is how YOU change our World to Peace!)

.

2a. You can also be seen as being bold and daring if you break the Virtues.

2b. Many modern groups (most notably youth) deliberately form their own identity by going against the Values of others.

(This causes their OWN depression, as they are intrinsically programmed to uphold the Virtues!)

2c. So be aware of the other person's real Values.

(use 1b to change their World and yours!)

.

.

.

3a. Focus on what you want, not what you do not want.

3b. CHOOSE to keep the VIRTUES,
or the vices,
and you reap all that YOU sow!

3c. If you now want to know what the vices are, then you are searching for something that you WILL find, and they WILL change YOU!
(Thank God for Diligence).

Yogi Sally Ann Slight

How Jesus Raised The Dead

Can You Keep A Secret?
(Praying is Time Travel)

...but beware what you Pray for,
because in all travel...

YOU COULD GET DELAYED
WITHOUT JESUS
AS YOUR GUIDE

Matthew 6:10

So, here you are visiting Dartmouth, in Devon,
and you have a friend or family member ...*(name)*...
back at home in ...*(town)*... who is not in good health!

Good Health!
...What is Good Health?

Good health is not bad health!
Good health is when you FEEL good, everything is working out well
for you, you are are fit and able to accomplish all the days tasks.

...What is bad health?
bad health is when you FEEL aches and pains, FEEL depressed,
FEEL heavy, everything does not seem to working out well for you,
you are not FEELING fit and able to accomplish all the days tasks,
stuff is falling out of your nose, you don't have a good thought in
your head, and even your head hurts.)

So perhaps you have come here on the bus,
IMAGINE the bus is your time machine...and you are
now in Dartmouth even before your friend is sick.!
You have come here to Dartmouth.....to go back in time.

(This is what we now call, Christian Science Fiction. Where we find
reality and imagination come together to create Miracles!
Believe in Vibration, not words).

So, before you left home, you found out that your friend was sick,
and you are obviously worried about them, yet you decide you are
still going on your visit to Dartmouth....and you come across this
writing, that has found you in a time of need, it is for you to stop
worrying about your friend, and as a prayer for your sick friend.

"So, why go back in time?....my friend is sick now!"

Well, your friend is sick because of something that happened in the past, and it has created this sickness in this moment....now!

A real prayer will eliminate the event from the past, to enable your friend to have good health now.....and that is called a miracle! We will revise the past event, and ensure that your friend will be well by the time you return home.

So you find that you are now here to 'Ask' for the Healing of your friend or family, and by the time you return home.... they are better,

and THEY KNOW NOTHING OF BEING IN BAD HEALTH!

This is the hardest part for you to understand.

"Why are they in good health when I return home?"

Well firstly, you 'asked'.....secondly, you made an 'effort' to get help .....and thirdly, you went back home 'expecting' everything to be better....didn't you?

....and then comes the part that only God Himself can sort out....He goes back in time and changes the event that created the bad health....isn't that wonderful?
This part of the information is between God and your friend, because only your friend really knows the reason why, and that is private between themselves.

The Power of a Miracle is Belief in them, and Belief in a Power greater than ourselves, and a Power that can change minds back to the purity in which they were created, just to bring Peace to a segment of time that also involves you, the friend.

And with Mercy, in your anguish for the welfare of your friend, we will perform the task you require, and all we ask is for your Belief and Trust in this matter.

There is in reality no bad health, only that which we Believe in, so that is why we require you to Believe that this matter is now resolved, and the matter is closed.

For you to keep peeking, or asking, to see if your friend is still in good health, is a lack of Faith on your part, therefore, you let yourself down, and your friend has to become ill again just because you cannot see them in good health.!...that is hardly fair is it?

They know nothing of bad health because all they know is Good Health, it is YOU who need someone to reflect your Beliefs upon....you Believe in bad health, therefore you need to see it, and when you see it you can then Believe in it......so if YOU could just STOP Believing in bad health, then you would only see Good Health.......and that is why this is so hard to understand.....because it means YOU HAVE TO CHANGE SO MUCH OF YOUR BELIEF SYSTEM TO ACCOMODATE SOMETHING YOU WANT TO BELIEVE IN.........phew!...and earn a living to pay your mortgage, no wonder we find it easier to Believe what everyone else Believes in.

It is now up to YOU and your FAITH in Jesus Christ and Father God that They can still work miracles.

Your Faith in Jesus Christ will be the bringer of the outcome you desire.
And to keep a secret is very difficult, especially when you are so happy to see your friend so well again.

And then your continued Faith is in keeping up the secret and they remain well...
How difficult is that going to be for you?

Your task will be exceptionally difficult, when more than one person is involved in the care and welfare of your friend, for they too see your friend in bad health, because that is what they too Believe!

I know, can you believe it! And after all your hard work in changing YOUR Beliefs, they go and let you down by not knowing about Good Health as well!
It's enough to make you want to not know this information isn't it?
Well, you can't go back now, you know it, and YOU will feel better for it at least.

It is down to you to share this knowledge with them, and then it is 'their' Belief that will also bring about the good health of your friend.

When you all understand that there is no bad health, only Good Health, will you all see the friend become better before your eyes.
It is what you WANT, not what you do not want, that you should Believe in.
Yet, you Believe in their bad health because that is what you see, their good health is hidden by yours and their Belief in bad health.

Yes, there are 2 ends to a stick, and it is your choice to name either end of the stick...but what if the stick is only a Good Health stick!?
There is not one end as good health, and the other end as bad health....there are just different levels of Good health!

> "We cannot solve our problems
> with the same thinking we used
> when we created them."
> Albert Einstein

Yes, there is a Law of Polarity and a Law of Opposites, and yet the Law of Gravity has only one outcome, everything that is dropped goes downwards....that is a God Law as it has only ONE OUTCOME! It is a Immutable Law.

The same is found with GOOD HEALTH, it is an Immutable God Law, and as such has only ONE OUTCOME.

Over the years you have been programmed to Believe in Good and bad Health, when really there is only Good Health, the bad only happens when you start to believe in bad things happening, and so you create in your outer experience all that you think and Believe that is within you!

None of the information that harms others, is any fault of your own, unless you now choose to NOT BELIEVE what you have just learnt here today.

Now, when you see your friend in bad health, you are then a witness to 'their' thoughts, for you have found the Belief that there is no bad health, so what you see is their thought forms being created in their experience, for them to experience, and you can now explain Good Health to them so they can get better faster, and be more careful in future......but that too is their CHOICE!

Please read on...

Well, once Jesus has said they are well,
THEY ARE WELL !
YOU CAN SEE, THEY ARE WELL!
and you don't have to keep the worry of, 'what if you change the situation again'!

By returning home on the bus and your friend is well,
THEN JESUS SAID YES !
If you return home and your friend is still unwell,
it is not your fault...

It is something your friend needs to sort out with Jesus and God themselves...!

You already KNOW Jesus can still Heal,
for you prayed for them, which was an act of FAITH,
you came all the way home on the bus praying that they would be well when you returned.

And if you tell them what you have done,
THEY now have to ASK Jesus to Heal their self.

This part is for them...

If you Believe in bad health, because you experience it...

Just look at this word...

BELIEVE = be LIE ve

bad health is a LIE !

It is all about CHOICE and the path you CHOOSE to experience, because without bad health you wouldn't know that you prefer Good Health, and without Good Health you wouldn't learn about CHOICE.
But, when it comes to Good Health, it just FEELS BETTER to BELIEVE in that!

BELIEVE in G(OO)D HEALTH.
It is as always a CHOICE to BELIEVE all that we want to experience, and then it feels better,
and when you FEEL BETTER you FEEL GOOD!

A God Law is a Good Law, it is Immutable, it doesn't change and it will always be, and when you understand that, then that is Goood!

gOd   = Omniscient
the Creator of all things, scient as in science.

gOOd   = Omnipresent
a gift, that keeps on giving, present as in gift, and as in Now.

gOOOd = Omnipotent
strength, with knowledge comes power, potent as in strength.

gOOOOd = Omnibus
Thank you

Now it is their turn to ASK !
Now expect a miracle!

Our Faith in Jesus is our own Faith and Belief.

*"The Law of Attraction is the reason for Beliefs to be perpetuated.
Step out of one Belief and create another, in perpetual perception."*

We can only guide and tell of how we have been helped
by Jesus in our own lives, and then it is up to the sick
person to BELIEVE and ASK Jesus themselves...!

But now the door is already open to Jesus' office,
for YOU have already knocked and ASKED for their
Healing in your prayers
and HE WAS LISTENING!.............(He always does!)

Say... "Thank you Jesus!"

Now thank Jesus for Healing YOU
and KNOW that you are well,
then you start your Journey of Faith.

*Your journey of Faith will bring you many answers to questions and
problems that you had in your past life. We call it a past life,
because now that you have found out about Godness, that life you
were living previously, is now just like a mist and fades away. All
the problems fade away, all those who hurt you fade away, and a
new brighter, lighter experience is being created around you every
day.*

*You will still retain the memories of the past life, and sometimes
they will overpower you and you will want to run back to them,
thinking that everything will have changed for their better too! But
until the past catches up with this new Good Life that you are now
experiencing, (Yes, it is Goood, and you will want to see more of it
soon) then you have to wait for them. It is still all about CHOICE.
And that is why so few people take this path, for they are separated
by Belief distance, but not by their thoughts of Love.*

If the past can continue to Love you, then you will always be connected and will meet again. Yet, if the past is filled with anger, hate, jealousy, condemnation and unforgiveness then there is a huge chasm that has been created between your two worlds, and unless the bridge of Forgiveness has been constructed by both parties, then that chasm cannot be crossed...and what a waste that really is...to not experience this great new life with your loved ones.

So just pray, and love, and smile, and know that everything is ok, and that one day, they too will forgive themselves, just as you have done.
And you have understood that they are now not needed to be forgiven, due to knowing our experiences are only of our own choosing, in what we are wanting to experience and live...
and what we CHOOSE to experience, we will experience.

Everyone has the right to experience everything, but we get tied into loyalty and obedience, to Laws that bind us to an experience that can bring us sadness and pain...just through our beliefs in duty!

Our true duty is happiness for ourselves, and then when we have understood that, we actually CHOOSE duty to serve others, then that is when we really enjoy serving, rather than when we feel we are made to, ordered to, or bound to serve.

Sometimes people take many years to find that they really enjoy serving others, and some times people find that by being ordered to serve was the best thing that could actually happen to them, and they really enjoy their duty.

We cannot judge others for the path that they have either chosen or are gifted to take, we can only find out for ourselves what our own personal journey should be.

And the reason we take it.?

Is to find comparison and in so doing, we have found our CHOICE and our LOVE of service to others.

.

.

.

We are so very thankful for your choice to take this path you are now on...
Yes, we are speaking this to Sally as she types it, yet, we are speaking this into the heart of everyone who reads it.

We are thankful to YOU for the choices you have made in your seeking of comparison.
YOU now know what you like and what you do not like.
So keep doing what you like, and do not do what you do not like.
If this upsets others on your journey, it is due to them not understanding the search for comparison and peace within themselves.

But, our dear friends, you will find that there are now more who do understand comparison, and that it was just YOU yourself that needed this information.
Many have already found their path of what they love to do...and it is good that they know this, for then there are no storms of emotion to have to deal with.
Storms of emotion create much in the way of disease and sadness, and so that is where you can then see that those people are actually on the path to finding their comparison.
So you can just bless them with your Peace of mind, and know that they too will find their way...just as you have...just as you have!

((We are so very thankful to you Sally, for sitting and being still, in order for you to type these words that will bring more peace and understanding to others who are walking the path you have walked...it is the same path...for there is only one path...the path of comparison.
And it is the knowledge of comparison that some others, who have understood the Goood, are trying to keep from your understanding...because it will not allow them to have you working to the way they want you to work...but until they understand that by giving you the choice to choose what part you play in their game of how to survive on this planet, then they too will still suffer the storms of emotion and sadness, which always brings disease.
Dis- ease, for they are not at ease.
We are at ease, when we are doing what we like and love to do.....when we feel trapped, by own own thoughts of entrapment, then we are not at ease)).

God does not allow anyone to be ill,
we are ill because we THINK and SAY we are ill...!
So stop saying you are ill and have FAITH you are
well.

And SMILE...
because Jesus died so He could see YOU SMILE!
(if that helps you and our Beliefs).

When you have FAITH in Jesus Christ and Father God,
you are always in Good Health...!
For YOU are then in a positive frame of mind.
And any time that YOU are negative is the 'sin' that
YOU have to overcome.
This is YOUR work...!
your thoughts are YOUR own responsibility.

ASK for help NOW!
...and Jesus Christ will be YOUR Guide and Saviour.

Go and get your ticket for the bus...
and LISTEN to HIM!

(or for more serious problems...perhaps you need to
travel further and faster...a bit like Superman flies
around the World to change time!).

You too can be a Super/wo/man ...get on the bus!
Keep positive,
Keep praying,
Keep knowing....................'He/She is well.'

Your FAITH adds to their own!

And have Faith in Jesus Christ,
and they will be well.

God Bless you Just like Jesus!
...a bit like Jesus, as you still have to get His help!

.
.
.
.
.

HOW JESUS RAISED THE DEAD

it happened because of all you read now!

this is Time Travel!

THANK YOU, JESUS

When You watch a news report,
or the papers You do read,
that is 'not' the harvest,
it is actually the seed!

They have written His-story,
although they say its News!
So what would have become of you,
if you had had the choice to choose?

You may look nice in that fur coat,
and in that big car that you drive,
but an Accident it never was,
as The Word, it never lies!

Perhaps you would still be home all safe,
and not in an Ambulance,
for every Report that they 'have' to write,
removes YOUR fighting chance!

"I 'want' to report a burglary,
I 'want' to report a murder,
I 'want' to get this off my chest,
and get MY story heard' er!"

Is Your story EGO,
or is it revenge or just a tiff?
for They will write down every Word,
before the body's even stiff!

You wonder why YOU gossip,
and all the harm that YOU do spread,
and as soon as You believe THEIR Word,
then that friend's as good as dead!

And negatives always return home,
and hurt YOU as You did they,
care fully with every Thought YOU Think,
and with every Word YOU say!

Remember, Jesus taught us,
to Forgive and Forget it all,
so You never experience what was writ,
and to Protect US as YOU fall!

That's how Jesus raised the dead!
for there was written a report,
and in 'The Bible' they were saved,
and so The Soul was always caught!

And thanks to His Disciples,
and writing His report,
He could escape from the big mess,
that His landing here had brought!

Do you think they over did it,
were they really that exposed?
Jesus thought they understood His Word,
before He decomposed!

But just like any story,
the ending must be writ,
so they brought Him back to Life again,
to re-enact ...and WE get hit!

Just sit and Think, and Think again,
before you grab the phone,
God Forgave YOU once before,
so resist, and in Peace condone.

For when YOU tell another,
of the problems that You've had,
then the seeds are sent back to the World,
and that's the experience, YOU've had.

So always keep YOUR big mouth shut,
when YOU feel another needs to Know,
and then Know Jesus WILL remove,
all those Thought seeds that YOU sow!

Your Thoughts they are YOUR demons,
and by 'telling' of YOUR woe,
the seeds of Thought land thick and fresh,
and in Good soil for them to grow!

So when YOU hear 'THEIR' demons,
'THEIR' pain and experience,
then the Armour You've been Given,
is YOUR Health as recompense!

No evil seed can harm YOU,
for Jesus has Your back,
and this battle that is raging,
is 'THEIRS' and all they lack.

Go figure this out for Yourself,
remember YOUR report,
an incident and They got paid,
although YOU sold Yourself real short!

Words written, are like Time Machines,
YOU created that bad smash,
YOU had a thought to make the News,
but what you really gained was cash!

Every Word that has been written,
creates with it a Past,
so only write the Truth of Love,
and Give info that will last!

Try this for Yourself today,
and now that 'YOU' really Know,
nothing can now harm YOU,
from all the spoken seeds YOU've sown!

You've planted very wisely,
within the minds of Good,
so now You have a worthy chance,
and be released, just as he should.

What YOU Think now is a warning,
be careful ....perhaps ....stop!
that Thought that YOU are having,
could produce another crop!

And now Your mind it ticks again,
thinking only of the Slave,
Just leave the planning up to US,
and be nicer to YOUR Brave!

Jesus taught YOU very well,
in 'How to Raise the Dead',
but when it's Time to let them go,
remember what WE said!

It's time to be a Healer,
and it's easier to see,
a Caring, Loving Smiler,
that Jesus wants You now to be!

You have the understanding,
You work better Undercover,
Your intellect has brought YOU down,
and now You are a better Mother!

The World's people are Your Family,
You see God within them all,
and YOU are there to help them,
and blessed by God's uncle!

Teach, 'How to be a Positive',
and Time Travel understand,
Your Journey here is over,
Please enjoy God's Given land.

Don't let them down,
because We Pray,
a Hero like YOU,
could save their Day!

by Yogi Sally Ann Slight

Hi kids...!!
Shamen info = past
Einstein info = future

Put them together and you find all the answers you will need to get you through the NOW!

Einstein told us about different dimensions,
different levels of existence,
all wrapped within one existence.
And so did the Shamen.

Therefore...
all the things you think are shadows, good and bad experiences that happen to you,
like sounds/smells/voices etc.
Are all on another level, of the existence that you are in NOW!

You only consider them bad, because you have no other information about them,
and you are protecting yourself...rightly so!

But they could also be great experiences that are about to happen, and you may miss out on them,
because of a fear based thought that you have not actually proven correct.

If you were pushed over by an invisible being, it is actually You with that other person on a different level (the next level down!),
and thankfully you being pushed over was just a small sample of the worse to come.

If you feel great about buying a lottery ticket (like you just know that this is the winning ticket)
...keep that feeling going until it manifests,
because that feeling is the actual feeling from you seeing that you have the actual ticket in your hand (or online if you do it that way).

Seeing shadow figures, is just you seeing figures that were there in the past levels or the future levels.

How does it feel?
It is always about the feeling

Shift to a better experience by raising your vibration.

You are protected by your 'knowing' that everything is ok.
'Knowing' is you programming every outcome as a success.

*"I just KNOW that everything I do will turn out for the best.
I don't know how it will happen, but I do KNOW everything is going
to be the best for me, my family, my friends, my town, my life...and I
am thankful that, I now KNOW this to be true."*

...and FEEL that it is true.

Just as you KNOW everyday the sun will rise,
(even if you do not see it)
you KNOW the sun is always there.

Now...FEEL you KNOW everything turns out the best for you,
...and only YOU can do this for yourself.
Because you are just catching up with all the good that is
happening to you...and for you...in the higher levels of your own
existence.
YOU ARE ALREADY THERE,
in that great dream you had for yourself.
But you allowed others and yourself, to talk yourself out of it and
settle in this lower dimension that you really are not happy in.

So, now get happy in the dimension you are already in,
be thankful you are here safe and well, housed and well fed.
Because it is all the good things that will link you to the higher
dimensions of your dream.

Like a puzzle, all the good things that you will take with you,
keep being thankful for them,
and allow them to lead you to your new dimension level.

Always be thankful for old friends...even if you left them suddenly.
You did that because you got a 'wiff' of another higher level of
dimension and only you alone, could go there.

You just wanted to experience it first...You can always return again!
Yes, it is your own journey, however much you love those with you.

When you want a higher dimension,
unless they want it too...they will remain in the lower dimension.

That is why you discuss things with your partner/family etc.

If you do not, you will travel alone to many different dimensions and
have many different experiences.

You get upset when a lover leaves you, because you do not know
how to speak of your dreams to them.
You think they will laugh at you, or leave you.
Well, they have left you anyway, and now you must move on to
another level and meet many more loves.

For once you have seen the higher level, you will find it very difficult
to stay in a lower level, even with the one you love.
You must tell them at once of your dream, or you will travel alone.

But, other loves also have other dreams, unless they have the
same dream as you...and how will they have the same dream?
You will tell them your dream...they will agree or disagree.
You will stay with them, or you will leave them to create the dream
yourself.

But you love them anyway.

And then...further down your life line...you meet them again.
You both took a different route, as they too wanted the same thing,
but only knew of a different way, due to their life training.

LOOK BACK ON YOUR LIFE...and these words,
"I don't know how it will happen,
but I KNOW everything will work out ok."

And has it?

Are you dead yet?

...then there is still time!

Love.
Love everyone,
Love everything,
Love.
...and things will shift again in your favour.
Everything will turn out for the best.

Sit, be still
and
KNOW...

EVERYTHING IS GOOD FOR ME...

NOW!

You are protected by the Law of Attraction on every level.

If the people that you might meet want to harm you,
and you want only good for yourself,
then you will always be on a level where good things happen and
bad things (the people who want to use you or harm you in any
way) do not happen...IT IS LAW.

KNOW THAT, You will never be...
where there is an accident that will include you.
where there is a violent crowd that might involve you.
where there is a violent partner who will harm you by word or deed.
where there is a violent family member who wants to harm you by
word or deed.
where there is earthquake, fire, storm, drought, war, or any
experience that may harm you in any way.

Whatever you FEEL is good for you...that is all you will experience,
because that is what you have chosen for yourself NOW!

It is always your choice,
and it is always the Law to bring you what you desire to experience.

You may not always understand it all,
but it is always a good experience. ....IT IS LAW!

"How I Found the Cure for My cancer."

on 4th November 2016.......even though I started on 12th May 2007.

Firstly, I became a Yoga Teacher at the Sivananda Yoga Ashram, on Paradise Island, Bahamas in May 2007.
Upon my return I made an effort to be with good people in Churches, lots of different Churches of different religions.
I sang alot in those Churches, as I had accessed during my Yoga Training, the gift of a beautifully high pitch of singing voice, and the acoustics are wonderful in some Churches.
Singing made me very happy, and so I could access the higher levels of information that the Superconscious offers everyone of us.

I found myself reading all sorts of Medical, Holistic, Religious and Self Help books and watching many YouTube information videos on all sorts of aspects of Healing modalities.....because.....

"The lips of wisdom are closed, except to the ears of understanding."
The Kybalion

I found more people on Facebook, who also wanted to learn more and improve themselves, and they also did a great job of improving me with their positive comments, thank you. (Yet I also found that some could actually take you off of your 'FOCUS' and onto theirs, until you clear yourself, and get back on your own track again!)

I found huge happiness in hanging out with all the old Scientists, Writers, Inventors, Artists, Architects, etc., in books and those great TV documentaries that are made about them.

Whatever is your interest, then keep everything on that subject around you, in you, and keep looking for more on that subject...never stop until you find what you are looking for...and if you look around your room and see posters of bands, lots of CDs and videos of music, then why aren't you singing or playing and instrument ????
There is a clue as to what you love, and your destiny...and you will find the answer to everything, when you really love it.

So why cancer?....surely you don't love cancer?

Well, 'I Love You', and I Love myself, and too many loved ones were leaving this planet sooner than they should.
So just like Dr Quincy, the Pathologist on TV, who wanted to find out how people died...I wanted to find out how to stop them from dying!!

So where do you start?

Believe in great lists of...
'How You Can Achieve Greatness In Your Life.'
here's two...

You are Life's Greatest Potential.

1. Find your passion and pursue it.
If you are going to find true abundance and prosperity in life, you MUST do what you love. You know what it is. There is that ONE thing that you want to do more than anything else. You are so passionate about it and you love it more than anything else.
Go after your dream.

2. Believe.
You must believe in your power, your potential, your abilities. BELIEVE IN YOURSELF. No action should take place without first intense belief. You can only act in accordance with the way you see yourself. If you don't have faith in yourself, you will never achieve your goals.

3. Lock the bridges...and give someone else the key.
(Knowledge is a lock and it's key is the question).
Don't give yourself a way out. If you know that there is NO OTHER OPTION than the one you really want, you will realize you HAVE to make this work, because there is no plan B. You are fully invested, and all in.

4. Study and model someone successful.

If you are looking to accomplish a certain goal, find someone who has already done what you want to do, and copy what they did to get there. Get your hands on everything you can to teach you what you need to do, and immerse yourself in all of it. Rather than spending time watching TV, or wasting time, spend every spare moment reading and studying all you can about others who have done what you want to do.

5. 'Focus in' on one thing at a time.

Don't spread yourself too thin. Just as the analogy of laying one brick at a time, you must focus in on one thing at a time. Choose what you want to do and try to put all your energy into that one thing.

6. Don't be typical.

You have heard the phrase, 'Results not typical'. Well, if you don't want typical results, then you need to go against the flow. 98-99% of people just go with the flow of life and accept ordinary results. Don't settle. Be different.

7. Protect your dream.

Don't let other people tell you what you can or can't do. People who believe they can't do something themselves, think that no one else can do it either. So, they will tell you it can't be done. Don't listen to them. They are not YOU.

And as I live in Dartmouth in Devon, UK,
home of the Britannia Royal Naval College,
I also found the Royal Naval Officers, 6 Core Values, very helpful.

The C2DRIL is....
Commitment,
Courage,
Discipline,
Respect, for self and others,
Integrity,
and
Loyalty......(but I like to say...*Love!*)

And eventually, these words do actually work for you.

You look back a year after first reading lists like these and they mean more to you, because you are keeping your Integrity, your Word to yourself, by not giving up!
Even though you don't understand at the time, what you are reading, being taught or watching...PERSIST!...and drip by drip your brain of understanding fills up.

And it feels so good to link knowledge together that comes from such different sources, yet, You can see the connection because You persevered.

And when you 'FOCUS' on one thing, and train like an Olympic Athlete, but with your brain muscle instead, you have to eat and drink the right things to bring optimum clarity to your Mind and body, but mainly because it is right and good to eat healthily.

There are many lists of greatness for you to find and follow...You will find the one that resonates with you, and it will bring you the success you desire in your life.

Take a small break here...Time for Tea!

But when I was just about to give up all hope, I was unemployed, all the bills were piling up and they wanted me to move out of my home...
I was given this...

A Prayer of Thanksgiving for Jude Thaddeus the Apostle of Hope.
Are you faced with a desperate situation?
The prayers to St. Jude help remind us that nothing is impossible with God, even help when you're at your wit's end.
This prayer, courtesy of the Dominican Shrine of Saint Jude Dominican Friars, is wonderfully straightforward:

Most holy Apostle, Saint Jude Thaddeus, friend of Jesus, I place myself in your care at this difficult time. Help me know that I need not face my troubles alone. Please join me in my need, asking God to send me:
consolation in my sorrow, courage in my fear, and healing in the midst of my suffering. Ask our loving Lord to fill me with the grace to accept whatever may lie ahead for me and my loved ones, and to strengthen my faith in God's healing powers.
Thank you, Saint Jude Thaddeus, for the promise of hope you hold out to all who believe, and inspire me to give this gift of hope to others as it has been given to me.
V. Saint Jude, Apostle of Hope
R. Pray for us!

And a few days later......

on the 4th November 2016, watching the YouTube information video,
https://www.youtube.com/watch?v=dWYOr1Z6WAE

Ho'oponopono, Dr Hew Len and Joe Vitale part 2
I Found the Cure for my cancer !

All the information I had collected since 2007 fell into place...
and I was peaceful, at last!

Phew!

...take a break!

Here is a very helpful little tip for you on your quest for either knowledge or success.....
Looking back now on that great day, I realized that the closer I came to the final information I required, the more I disliked Joe Vitale!

Every email and video he sent me annoyed me, and I switched him off.

Then on the 23rd October 2016, I was having a particularly happy day so I opened one of his emails, and he had written the kindest and most loving words that I had read in years.

Here they are....

You are a divine creation.
You are woven with perfection and gifted with power.
You are beauty and love in human form.
You are a true artistic expression.
You are the creator of infinite designs.
You are the force of a thousand hearts.
You are a gift to the world.
All you have to do is see it.
See it.
Love, Joe
P.S. There is no limit to who you are. Zero limits.
Only the limits you hold onto.
Let go.

And then Joe reminded me....
Two years ago, I heard about a therapist in Hawaii who cured a complete ward of criminally insane patients, without ever seeing any of them. The psychologist would study an inmate's chart and then look within himself to see how he created that person's illness. As he improved himself, the patient improved.

I had always understood "total responsibility" to mean that I am responsible for what I think and do. Beyond that, it's out of my hands. I think that most people think of total responsibility that way. We're responsible for what we do, not what anyone else does.

The Hawaiian therapist who healed those mentally ill people can teach you about an advanced new perspective about total responsibility. His name is Dr. Ihaleakala Hew Len.

He explained that he worked at Hawaii State Hospital for four years. That ward where they kept the criminally insane was dangerous. Psychologists quit on a monthly basis. The staff called in sick a lot or simply quit. People would walk through that ward with their backs against the wall, afraid of being attacked by patients. It was not a pleasant place to live, work, or visit. Dr. Len said he never saw patients. He agreed to have an office and to review their files. While he looked at those files, he would work on himself. As he worked on himself, patients began to heal.

"After a few months, patients that had to be shackled were being allowed to walk freely," he said. "Others who had to be heavily medicated were getting off their medications. And those who had no chance of ever being released were being freed."

"Not only that, but the staff began to enjoy coming to work. Absenteeism and turnover disappeared. We ended up with more staff than we needed because patients were being released, and all the staff were showing up to work."

We asked, "What were you doing within yourself that caused those people to change?"
"I was simply healing the part of me that created them," he said.

And so I once again enjoyed reading what he wrote to me, and once again all the correct information I had asked for was gently guided to me.
I just had to be open enough to see it.

*...take a break!

When you hear the story of the Grandmother and her grandson who has the throat cancer, at the 20minute mark on the video, you will want to watch the whole video to get the information you require, and best to start with video One in the series.
Remember, if you don't understand the information on the video (just as many in the audience do not understand Dr Hew Len as he explains to them), keep this in Mind, C2DRIL, and immerse yourself in it again and again, leave it for a few weeks and then come back to it again....you will be so glad you did!

*...take a break!

Keep saying, "I am sorry, Please forgive me, Thank you, I love you" to allow the Divine to clear your chaos and cut your ties to dis-ease.
Let go and let God.

Be a Zero Hero...
an O mniscient, O mnipotent, O mnipresent Healthy Being.

"*The lips of wisdom are closed, except to the ears of understanding.*"
The Kybalion..........(again these words keep you searching for more).

.

On the 3rd November 2016, I had to conquer another fear, the one about telling people the title of my newest book!.......(although I had the same fear when I wrote, "How Jesus Raised the Dead.").

So, at the Ladies Lunch in the Dartmouth Yacht Club, I told them of my newest book, and they asked me for it's title. I stammered and reminded them of how everyone persecuted Charles Darwin and the other great finders of Truth, but now teach their work in Schools, and to accept that perhaps it could be true what I had found as Truth. They said they understood and so I felt confident enough to tell them, deep breath.......
"How The cancer Fell Out Of Me," I said.

.

.

.

.

.

Yes, there was about this much space between their next breaths, but the first words mentioned was about Lawyers and claims that what I had told them did not work, and where was the proof?

I enlightened them with the fact that this information was in books and on videos and is out there for everyone to find, my book was just to bring people the information and for them to read, watch and say the words required.

Not only I have found this information, but so have many others, and perhaps the title of this book will bring more readers to wellness.

As for proof, why waste time looking for evidence, do the simple task that this video asks you to do, to save your Life, and that of your family members.

It worked for me!

.

.

.

The rest of the lunch conversation was about the weather. I understand now that this had to happen as I didn't know it all yet!

The best evidence I ever found, is in The Bible. (NIV)

"FATHER, FORGIVE THEM, FOR THEY DO NOT KNOW WHAT THEY ARE DOING" Luke 23:34
Is because of the programming.....just keep cleaning your mind, with the words from Ho 'oponopono.

Genesis 50:17 'This is what you are to say to Joseph: I ask you to forgive your brothers the sins and the wrongs they committed in treating you so badly.' Now please forgive the sins of the servants of the God of your father." When their message came to him, Joseph wept.

HO'OPONOPONO CLEARS THE SINS OF THE FATHERS/
ANCESTORS THAT ARE CREATING DISEASE IN THE CHILDREN...
WORRY IS TRANSFERRED.
PRAY FOR YOURSELF AND TAKE 100% RESPONSIBILITY BY SAYING...

"I am sorry, Please forgive me, Thank you, I love you."

AND CLEAN THE CHAOS OF THE SUBCONSCIOUS PHYSICAL MEMORY. CHOOSE TO CLEAR THE CONSCIOUS MENTAL MEMORY AND BECOME ALIGNED WITH GOD AGAIN...TO BE INSPIRED AND HEALTHY.

Saying, "I LOVE YOU" is You knocking on Divinities door.

and when you understand that, YOU WANT TO MAKE AMENDS FOR WHATEVER IS GOING ON IN ME, THAT I EXPERIENCE MY FAMILY MEMBER HAVING (whatever disease).

Say now,
"I AM SORRY,
PLEASE FORGIVE ME,
THANK YOU,
I LOVE YOU."

Let go, and let God fix it.

Why Ho Oponopono ?

"I AM SORRY..."
because I was not conscious of my thoughts.

"PLEASE FORGIVE ME..."
I have been so unconscious, because everything I have in my Life, I was not aware that I had that in me, because I was unaware of my programming, and that of my ancestors, is that which I am now experiencing.

"THANK YOU..."
to the Divine, God, Universe, Source.
Thank you for erasing my negative programming and blessing me with your Inspiration.

"I LOVE YOU."
for taking such good care of me, my family and my ancestors.

What is Real?
That, that never changes!

I am......
I am is the name of God.

So when I say, "I am healthy",
the name of God has been used to open the door to good
health.

The same goes with when you say,
"I am ...*negative word...*"

You will be gifted with all that you ask...
whether you knew it or not!

Now you know!

"IF THAT'S SO, THEN WHY DID MY DAUGHTER'S CHILD DIE OF CANCER?"

or

"This is the book I wish I had read BEFORE my friend died of cancer.'

There she stood, behind the tea counter, as I placed my order for a cup
of Earl Grey tea.
"Is that strong enough for you?"
she said, as she tried to remove the teabag from the cup.

"Let it brew for a little longer."
I said,
"Earl Grey tends to need a little longer in the cup."

"They make those bags out of hemp don't they, or is it plastic? There is
so much plastic in us these days, all those bottles floating in the sea,
plastic in the fish, plastic in our food, plastic giving us cancer."
she said.

"And plastic in ladies chests!"
I laughed,
"But I find that if you don't worry about those sort of things, life is
generally ok. You don't get cancer if you don't think about it and worry
about it." I said, wondering if I might be wrong, yet still clinging to
the knowledge that, I am right.

She stood there, and stared at me straight in the face and said,
"Then why did my daughter's kid die of cancer?"

.

.

.

.

.

So, you either tell her why, straight, and know that she won't believe it, (*as it would involve her changing her opinion very quickly, and without the luxury of time and inclination to learn, and to understand that there is so much truth out there that you really have to look for*), or you change the subject and say to yourself again,
'Now is the time to write that blasted book!'

.

.

.

"The tea is lovely, thank you."
I smiled and paid her for the tea, and vibrated a kind hearted peace towards her.

She carried on happily serving the next customer as I walked away, not even acknowledging the conversation we just had together.
"You did it again"
'Did what?'
"You got your information. You asked and we gave it to you. Now, what are you going to do with it?"
'I asked?'
"You sent out a thought, we felt it, and we had to find a way to give you an answer, from a being that was receptive enough to allow us to step in and converse with you, and since you are very young to this understanding, we have you travel, and meet strangers who will give you the information you require."

.......(just then the song from Dio flowed into my mind, "Don't talk to strangers, they are an evil drug, to make you loose your mind).
'Rubbish! She is just a normal unknowing human who wanted to know, in the simplest way possible.'

'And young? I am in my 50s!'

"Consider 'new' then, rather than young in your earth years."

'So I am new to this?'

"Yes"

'What is this?'

"Understanding.....of who you are."

'A being who is receptive?'

"Not any more! but she is..... and Yes, just as you were! You were open enough for us to speak through you to others, so they would also hear information that they needed to bring them more understanding and help them on their journey to happiness."

.

.

.

So, why do kids die of cancer?

"Let's start at the beginning shall we!"

Mummy and Daddy decide they want to make a baby and so Daddy plants a seed in Mummy's tummy and a baby starts to grow in Mummy's tummy garden.

Now you are being silly!

"And the word silly has ILL in it, so they wILL understand!"

The seed is a cell made from the Daddy and it inserts itself into a cell of the Mummy, the cells form more cells that grow into a baby inside the Mummy.

The cells are genius and know exactly what to do to grow into a baby.

The cells are good cells and they know exactly what to do.
The cells are genius and know exactly what to do.
...the cells know what to do! OK! They know exactly what to do!

The Mummy on the other hand, is also a group of cells that are genius.
But the Mummy sometimes listens to her brain, her partners brain, her
friends and families brains, and they discuss the programming that
they have downloaded throughout their life times, rather than be at
peace with the pregnancy process and allow the cells to create in
tranquil perfection, knowing that all is well, and that the baby is a
mass of cells that are genius, and are growing in perfection to be
perfection.

Because they are!
"Yes, because they are!"

But sometimes the Mummy and Daddy fear the future.
They read all sorts of stories about diseases in children that are true,
because they have happened, so they are true, to the people they have
happened to...but not to the new Mummy and Daddy...yet!

But the more that the Mummy and the Daddy, and the Family and
friends, keep reading about, and watching videos about, and talking
about, all the sad disease stories.
And the more that they believe that they happen, because they do
happen, and so they are true, and they think that they should keep
informed of all the things that could go wrong in the pregnancy, they
keep reading, watching and talking about all the diseases that the
child could get before it is born, after it is born and as it is growing
up.

Then that is what we can expect for the new baby, even before it is born!

Even before the Mummy and Daddy plant a seed in the Mummy's tummy garden?
"Yes, that is true, even before then."

We have so much access to so much information nowadays, but are we accessing the correct information?
"Well the disease information is correct if you want a child with a disease."

How about accessing healthy information that keeps your child perfect?
"The cells are already perfect! They know what to do! Helpful kind information is also out there to be found, but you like to live in fear it seems!"

You may not do it consciously, like choose what coffee you prefer. You think coffee makes you happy, so you chose to eat food that you think makes you happy and you drink drinks that you think makes you happy. They please the senses, until the senses are not pleased.
But when it comes to Health you read, watch and speak about subjects that do not make you happy!

But I must be informed.

"WHY?"

So that I will know what it is when it happens.

"So you being knowledgeable is more important than your child's health?"

If it keeps them alive!

"Then don't read, watch or talk about disease and death if you want your children to stay alive, before it is even born!"

It is a Law, you attract what you think, speak and put your focus upon. It is how big businessmen get wealthy, and also how healthy people stay healthy.
Focus on what you do want. Speak about what you do want. Write about what you do want. Read about what you do want."

When you are reading about sickness, sadness and death, you are placing yourself at the same level as that you are focusing upon!
A very low vibration which will bring you more of the same.

When you read about happiness, good health, prosperity and success, well blow me down, you get more of the same!

The Law of Attraction, it is a marvellous Law that is given to us to keep us healthy.
Along with the other Laws which keep all aspects of our lives in the good and abundant state that we are meant to be in.

We have a choice?
"Some do not even realize that they have a choice."

Well, now you do.

And now you have some hard work to do, in choosing the thoughts that will keep you and your family healthy and living more prosperous lives.

Every thought of disease, sadness and sickness creates another layer, another step backwards from your good life.

How do you know when you are reading, writing and speaking about the wrong things that harm you and your family?
"You feel bad when you speak them, read them and write them."

Your emotions are like your internal SatNav that guide you back on the right road to prosperity and good health.
When you ARE happy, it is due to you being aligned with your higher self, and either thinking a good thought, remembering a happy occasion and CHOOSING to be happy, when everyone else around you is sad or sick, or poor.

You will have also been saving in your Happiness Bank as it were!
The more you put into it, and with increasing interest, the more you get out of it.
But, the more sad, sick and angry thoughts you deposit in your Happy Bank the deeper you get into debt, and all those sickness thoughts and stress that they bring!

There are lots of ways to be and keep happy, you just have to 'want' to find them...(Smiling helps).
Just the same way you wanted to find out about the information that makes you sad, sick and poor...and you didn't even know it was building up more of the same inside of you and your family.

So, you are saying that her daughters child died of cancer, because her Mother and Father, her friends and even she worried about it, talked about it, thought about it?

"Yes, that is true!"

And by doing so, they also made the child believe there was something wrong.
And so her body acted accordingly, and gave them what they all wanted, to be proven right, and that there was something wrong.

Well you know they didn't want it, but the Law of Attraction gives you what you focus upon, and they were all focusing upon sickness and future death, instead of being thankful for happiness and good health.

And now that YOU know about the Law of Attraction, so many others will know about it, and that means so many others won't go through the same pain and hurt, and keep hurting others with their sad stories and belief in sickness.
Just because it happens in others, that do not know how to control their thoughts and words, does not mean that it happens to you. That is what we would really like you to know at this time.

.

.

.

.

Thank you for reminding me that I had to write the book.

"You are welcome.
Peace be with you."

BI-POLAR?
...How to help yourself with Happiness

Why would a medical term incorporate an old Holistic Principle ? Unless medicine is acknowledging that the Mind and Body must be in harmony, to create perfect good health.
Mental induction means that mental states may be produced by 'induction' from others.

So a higher mental vibrational rate may be communicated to another person, elevating the polarity of that person's mental state.

This is how the majority of 'mental treatments' occur.

....BUT !

This is where you really need to understand the Law of Polarity...

While you are busy raising everyone else's mental state to a higher vibration and making them happy...

Do you know who is looking after your 'own' mental state???

ONLY YOU!!!

This is where some people claim that their energy has been taken from them, by energy vampires! And so they complain and blame someone else, instead of understanding that they are 'giving' their energy, and they haven't yet found a way to keep the energy flowing. So they say they feel 'drained'. And by saying it, they are focusing on lack, rather than, 'Oh, now I have to get some more?'

Only you can raise your own mental vibrations to a higher level, so perhaps this is the first time you have understood what it is you can do...

Then now is where you will gain some relief and happiness, for knowledge is power... is happiness... is raising vibration!

Don't you always find you are happier when you get the answer to a problem that has been bothering you for some time?....*like years!?*

And lower vibrations are depression, and depression will never give you an answer because...

"We cannot solve our problems with the same thinking we used when we created them." Albert Einstein

...and...

"When the solution is simple, God is answering." Albert Einstein

So, now you need to learn how to raise your vibrations to get the answer to your question...just like Einstein did!

...or just to be happy enough to get you out of your depression.

Start with a SMILE...

even if, and you may have to, force one onto your face.

For the Mind doesn't know why you are smiling, it is just reacting to the receptors that are pushed, when the face is placed in the SMILE position.

It takes a lot of work to SMILE...and yes, it is easier to be a sad face, but with all things that are worth attaining, you have to work at it, to get what it is that you require...and in this instance it is HAPPINESS.

Happiness raises your vibrations, and then the good stuff starts happening in your life again.

If good stuff has been happening whilst you are sad...

did YOU create it??

....or have you got good friends and family who were happy enough to create it for you?

It is all about choice, but sometimes, *(and we are talking to the Bi-Polar in you again)*, you didn't even know you had a choice!

Well, now you do!

Sadness is not something that you HOPE will go away, or you pop a pill to make it go away.

That is useful until you understand how to do it yourself. Then you can slowly decrease use of the medication, and your body can remove the toxins that are not necessary for your happiness.

Actually, sadness is a gift!

And when you start looking at all negative qualities as gifts, rather than something to be got rid of, as they are only the opposite of a positive quality. You will be able to feel lighter and happier from this understanding and that you now know about comparison.

Lack of knowledge is like carrying a heavy load, it weighs you down until you can bear it no longer and you get even sadder.

So, SMILE........NOW....................and you will feel lighter.

Your body will try to stop you...

Your mind will try to stop you...

But you are now like an Olympic Athlete...

who gets up at 3am every morning to run and train before they go to work...

who trains in their lunch break...

who trains before they go home to feed the family...

who trains after they have fed the family...

who knows how important a good sleep is for you when you are training!

...if they can do it.....so can YOU!

(you just have a different event to train for than them, but the training is still the same!)

...and YOU WILL WIN GOLD IN SMILING!

When you train yourself, and have Faith in yourself, and your ability...to SMILE.

AND YOU REALLY ARE THE WORLD'S GREATEST SMILER!

Keep up the good work...we are all so proud of you.

Thank you...
Yogi Sally Ann Slight

.

.

.

Yogi Sally Ann Slight
Dartmouth
Devon
UK

Yoga Life Coach & Good Health Motivator.
Yoga Siromani taught at Sivananda Ashram, Bahamas 2007.
Masseuse/Motivator to EDDIE KIDD (after his accident),
and the SUPER BIKERS at BRANDS HATCH Race Circuit, Kent,
Life Coach/Motivator to Servicemen with addictions & P.T.S.D.
and gives Solutions to questions on Facebook.

Just as Yoga Asana classes keep your body flexible and healthy,
you also need a flexible mind to regain strength and happiness to
improve your life situation.

To understand your emotions and feelings, and how to change
them, will bring you great success in reaching any of your life
ambitions or embarking upon a change in career...or enabling you
to cope with loss or suffering from depression.

Health has a root, and the root is based within the mind, and when
you are understanding your emotions you can then weed out
sickness and negative paths and return your life of happiness.

You have the CHOICE to be happy or sad!...it is a good habit that
will give you the understanding to regain, and maintain, your health,
happiness and success again.

...and don't forget...that I too, was just like YOU !

www.ingramcontent.com/pod-product-compliance
Lightning Source LLC
Chambersburg PA
CBHW031626040426
42452CB00007B/688